Acclaim for Richard Lischer's

Stations of the Heart

"An inspirational memoir. . . . Lischer is a fine writer—
self aware, humorous and unstinting in describing
the outrage of a son dying before his father."
—*The Toronto Star*

"A fond view of a father-son relationship and a loving
tribute from a minister to a son who chose a different
spiritual path in his life and to his death."
—*Kirkus Reviews*

"By the story's close, you'll have laughed, prayed,
shaken your fist at the sky, and wept along with
the author and his family. Lyrical, wise, and full of
warmth, *Stations of the Heart* accomplishes what only
the best memoirs can: it bears witness to the unimag-
inable and gives voice to the inarticulable."
—David McGlynn, author of *A Door in the Ocean*

"As he grieved over the loss of his son, Richard Lischer gradually discovered that he had been given a new role—as the interpreter of his own son's death. In this tender and loving book, Lischer does indeed become an interpreter, not only of his son's death but also of the fragile and beautiful relationships that make life both a peril and a gift for us all. Lischer is a faithful witness whose truthful and searing testimony evokes memory, provokes tears, and finally points powerfully toward hope."

—Thomas G. Long, author of
What Shall We Say?: Evil, Suffering, and the Crisis of Faith

Richard Lischer

Stations of the Heart

Richard Lischer has taught for more than thirty years at Duke Divinity School. His many books include the prizewinning *The Preacher King: Martin Luther King, Jr. and the Word That Moved America* and an earlier memoir, *Open Secrets: A Memoir of Faith and Discovery*. He and his wife live in Orange County, North Carolina.

Stations of the Heart

Stations of the Heart

PARTING WITH A SON

Richard Lischer

VINTAGE BOOKS

A Division of Penguin Random House LLC

New York

FIRST VINTAGE BOOKS EDITION, MARCH 2015

Copyright © 2013 by Richard Lischer

All rights reserved. Published in the United States by
Vintage Books, a division of Penguin Random House LLC, New
York, and distributed in Canada by Random House of Canada,
a division of Penguin Random House Ltd., Toronto. Originally
published in hardcover by Alfred A. Knopf, a division of
Penguin Random House LLC, New York, in 2013.

Vintage and colophon are registered trademarks of
Penguin Random House LLC.

Pages 253–54 constitute an extension of this page.

The Cataloging-in-Publication Data is on file at the
Library of Congress.

Vintage Books Trade Paperback ISBN: 978-1-101-91047-4
eBook ISBN: 978-0-307-96054-2

Book design by Soonyoung Kwon
Author photograph © Les Todd

www.vintagebooks.com

Printed in the United States of America
10 9 8 7 6 5 4 3 2 1

What is elegy but the attempt
To rebreathe life
Into what the gone one once was
Before he grew to enormity.

Come on stage and be yourself,
The elegist says to the dead. Show them
Now—after the fact—
What you were meant to be:

The performer of a live song.
A shoe. Now bow.
What is left but this:
The compulsion to tell.

—MARY JO BANG,
from "The Role of Elegy"

The Fountain

I

Seven years ago, on the thirteenth day of April, my son called to tell me his cancer had returned. He was a grown man, but he told me his news like a boy. He said, "Hey, *Dad,* where's Mom?" You would have thought he had just put a dent in the family's new car or failed a final exam. He might have been in a little trouble and wanted his mother to buffer the rough edges. He said they had found tumors in quite a few places in his body, on his liver, chest, side, and more. Then he asked me to come to him. And that was all.

I was not expecting the call. But then you never are. You are never adequately braced with feet planted and stomach muscles clenched. Just when you should have been steely-eyed, you were caught looking away, distracted by a passing thought, and now it is too late. A police car with its rotating blue light—why in *my* driveway? An envelope marked "Personal" from someone you don't know. A stranger in uniform who doesn't say hello, but asks you who you are and where you live.

A phone call from your son.

A familiar voice emerges from a piece of inexpensive black plastic. The voice has no body, and yet it makes a claim as firm and authoritative as flesh. It says "Hey, *Dad*" with an end stress on *Dad* that has always and in every circumstance meant trouble. "Hey, *Dad,*" and ordinary time stands still and the room begins to turn while you wait for the rest of the sentence to do its work. "Why don't you come over to 2 K," it says. The ruin in his voice becomes the new truth in your life, and your old life, the only one you have ever known or wanted, simply vanishes.

We addressed each other with an economy of passion, as men will do when they are trying to curtail a feeling, as if what had just passed between us was a new piece of information and not a revelation. We spoke as if the end of the ages had not yet come upon us. I do remember later that evening sobbing into the bedroom wall and hitting it hard with my fist. "It is a robbery!" I cried. But at the moment of his call, there was shockingly little to say. Our brief conversation left no room for misunderstanding and no remainder of options to be sorted out later. I pressed *End* on my cell phone and began to make my way from the first floor of the hospital to the clinics in an adjoining building.

Even as I was running down corridors, weaving around gurneys, and fumbling with my cell phone to call my wife, something new and forbidden was forming in my imagination. My eyes had begun to burn with a future I was never intended to see. In an ordered world, beginnings and endings are off-limits. A parent is not designed to comprehend the child's life in its entirety, any more than the child is meant to experience the parent's early days or youthful indiscretions. It is a sensible arrangement. Children are not permitted to witness the passions that produced them, and parents are not allowed to observe their children's final hours.

It follows that a father has no business writing a book about his son's death. This is proper work for sons, perhaps when they themselves are graying and secure in the world—to sum up, round off, and memorialize their fathers. These sons write out of a profound sense of duty toward the generation that preceded them and formed them.

With me it is different. My son has become one of the fathers to me.

When I survey my dad, he is always old; he appears as solid and factual as history. But when I steal a glance at my son, what I feel is closer to enchantment, which is a more complicated subject than history, and more compelling. When I look over my shoulder expecting to face the stable and monumental figure of my father, I see an open-faced boy smiling back at me.

He was so young and inexperienced he thought he had discovered a new way to die. All my wife and I could do was keep him company and follow him on what he somewhat dramatically called his "new path." His new way, which was actually a very old way, carried him beyond the stars to the very origins of his universe and to the source of everything he loved. We traveled the path with him, but at a respectful distance behind him, learning from him and trusting him to show us the way. The last leg of his trip took him exactly ninety-five days. We never imagined how much grace would be required for so brief a journey. Now we rely on it every day.

It wasn't until he got sick that I walked the Stations of the Cross for the first time. Until then, I had never thought of them as anything other than a ritual for pious Catholics and a few venturesome Protestants. But as his illness wore on, the Stations began to loom in my imagination, perhaps because cancer itself leads you from one obligatory shrine to the next. It is a disease that teaches incrementally.

In most churches the Stations are so graphic in their depiction of Jesus' suffering that they leave little to the imagination: he staggers, he falls, he bleeds, he dies. The ribs protrude from his corpse like piano keys. This is what a young man's death looks like. A few summers ago, when I was teaching at Saint John's University in Minnesota, I noticed something different about the Stations in the abbey church. They were nothing more than plain crosses cut into the granite pavement. They were not designed to restrict the imagination but to expand it and make it more inclusive. When you stand or kneel on one of these cross-shaped slits, as brutal in their own way as the medieval gore they were meant to replace, they remind you that anyone's pain, including your own, can find a place in something larger than itself.

It all begins with the Stations. You have to make every last one of them. You have to go with him for his labs and scans, hang out in the coffee shops, walk the dogs, listen to the same old stories, share the same old jokes, and carry on with him for hours about nothing in particular. And when things get serious, you have to keep your part of the bargain and try not to cry. When he wants to talk about God, you have to hide your own damaged faith, clear your palate of clichés, and find a witness deep within yourself.

Some pretending is involved. You have to nod sagely when he says, "Time is irrelevant," even when you have secretly begun to date your own life from a single telephone call. You have to pretend that you are not counting out his days like silver dollars.

All this requires a lot of love, and love is a harsh comforter, because only love makes genuine loss possible. You can't lose what you never loved.

A man said to my wife and me, "We can give your son back to you." "No," she said, and nearly took the poor man's head off. We were sitting in a richly appointed office around a mahogany desk. "You will *not* give our son back to us." It was a low point. Still, the man was only following a natural if professional instinct, the human instinct to keep, hold, and restore. It's what the poet Julia Kasdorf had in mind when she wrote, "Grieving a loss is not only the process of letting go, but it is also the process of keeping, like writing, through acts that allow you to continue to consummate the other."

Those who grieve have no illusions about denying death or making it into a beautiful experience. We only want to remember in a saving way so that something whole and complete may come into view. To remember in this way is the work of God. My religious tradition calls it Resurrection. If you obey the human instinct to keep and to consummate, you are doing the work of God whether you know it or not. Remembering is a sacred act.

And a saving act. "How can we know the way?" a skeptic once asked Jesus. The time comes when everyone repeats the same bewildered question with the same shattered implication: there *is* no way. And even if there is, how can anyone know it? My son asked the question, and in my own good time I asked it too. Neither one of us ever got a straight answer, but we were both shown a path. His was marked "To Blessedness." Mine was a bit more obscure and overgrown, but it eventually took me to a better place as well. It led me from the bitter gall of losing him to something like a settled sorrow. From "It is a robbery" to "He was my son, and I give thanks for him."

2

His mother and I decided to call him Adam because it was a good strong name. Our choice of a name was something of an inside joke. During each of Tracy's two pregnancies her mother, Nina, repeatedly cautioned us against flimsily named offspring. She reminded us that later in life such unfortunate children have nothing to stand on. Never mind that she named her own child Tracy, not after a biblical matriarch but after a character in a movie played by Katharine Hepburn. Still, "Pick a good strong name," she insisted. So we did. In the book of Genesis the name Adam means "mankind," the corporate representative of all humanity. We named him Everyman. Adam also means "dirt," which is one of the many little puns the Bible is full of. Since we were living out in the country in those days, among farmers who knew the value of good soil, the name seemed right to us.

He lived up to his humanity on the day he was born.

He turned yellow with jaundice and blue with a pulmonary obstruction, his ribs heaving and his chest shuddering with every breath. His airway was reamed out twice, and a nurse wrote, "Baby fought tube et gagged et spit." When I first met him he was lashed to his incubator by wires, tubes, and lines, like a small animal caught in a net meant for larger prey. Only three hours old and governed by forces beyond his control, he had already assumed what W. H. Auden called the "human position." It would be another six days until the nursing notes pronounced him "pink."

For his discharge photo one of the nurses parted his hair on the side and did a comb-over. In it he looks like a tired old man. For the record, he is not pink; he is yellow.

We brought him home from the hospital to a white bungalow-style parsonage on the Illinois prairie across the Mississippi from St. Louis. The house stood no more than fifty feet from a red-brick Lutheran church with a tall, peeling steeple. At the very top of the steeple one of the arms of the cross was broken and dangled like the wing of a wounded bird.

We lived at the junction of a soybean field and a graveyard. A dense heath plunged into a ravine behind the church, then rose and plunged again until it finally disappeared into a den of thorn trees.

On the morning he was baptized, the fields on each side of the church and across the road were frozen. The bramble bushes in the heath blazed in the winter sun, as delicate and brittle as glass. Inside, the church felt as cold as it was outside, but the light streaming through the Trinity window above the altar made his baptism glow like a scene from the Old Masters. Since I was the pastor in this out-of-the-way place, it was I who baptized him. He was one of my 262 parishioners. One of the lessons for the day was from the Letter of James: "Every good and perfect gift is from above, coming down from the Father of lights with whom there is no variation or shadow due to change."

Adam wore the same baptismal dress his sister, Sarah, had worn sixteen months earlier and that I had worn at my baptism and my father before me. It is a flowing white cotton shift with an inset and garniture of embroidered lace. My grandmother made it in 1910 when she was twenty and could not have imagined that my father would be her only child or that the dress she was making would outlive him by generations.

As usual, our memory of a sacred occasion is blurred by trivia. I have no recollection of the hymns or the sermon that I preached that morning, but I do remember that the toilets in the basement froze and my father-in-law was wearing a cashmere coat in a country church. We have a few murky photos of the dress, and I remember the weird combination of tortellini soup, fried chicken, and beer afterward at a nearby restaurant—the culture of the sacrament, you might say—but I don't remember being penetrated by its grace.

Did any of the perfect sentences from the baptismal rite register on us? Fortunately, baptism is one of the few occasions where memory and feelings do not matter. It is even more elemental than that, as the poet Philip Larkin attests:

If I were called in
To construct a religion
I should make use of water.

I can tell you that the water was cold, and I am certain the right words were spoken because they came from the official book. Tracy and I had next to nothing between us in those days—I made $530 per month—but with my first church and these two babies and the many blessings hidden in this water, we felt absurdly rich.

We were an odd little group that morning, made up mainly of farmers along with steelworkers and mechanics, a couple of teachers, and a preacher and his wife. Among us we harbored the even odder belief that our ceremony provided a template of meaning for the child's entire life. Adam's name was a clue. The ritual asks you to imagine that the man of earth, in this case a sleeping child in his father's lace dress, is being drowned with Jesus in order to be raised with him to perpetual light. The child begins life's journey with a dramatic funeral— his own. Baptism is a way of saying, *Adam is dead. Long live Adam!*

After the water I took him in my arms and marked his forehead and chest with the universal sign of suffering. And this *is* something I wish I could feel and remember. I wish the muscles in my arm and the wall of my chest were still programmed to register the weight of his flesh on mine. How he felt to me when we put his name in a bottle, set it adrift, and abandoned him to God. I said, "Richard Adam, the Lord preserve your going out and your coming in from this time forth and forever more." And everyone in the frigid little church cried Amen.

We didn't stay long on the Illinois prairie. First assignments are like that in most churches. The congregation teaches the young pastor everything it knows in short order, and he and his family move on to "a wider field of service." Our loneliness out there must have weighed on us, but what we remember most about our time in the country are the moments of freedom found only in remote places, when your isolation and loneliness remind you that you are a family and you will survive as a family.

Sometimes the four of us would crowd onto the porch swing on the front of the house and listen to the creepy sounds that came out of the tall corn at dusk. On the same porch swing Tracy taught the children hymns from the Lutheran hymnal and songs from Broadway musicals, and the three of them would fill the sky with "Holy, Holy, Holy" and "I'm Getting Married in the Morning." After breakfast, Tracy and I would drink our coffee under the oak tree out back while we watched the kids run wild in the cemetery behind the house. They played hide-and-seek among the headstones and sang like rock stars from the tops of the graves.

In the spring the ushers would open the church doors after services, creating a framed, oceanic view of the fields across the road, and I would greet the people with Adam standing between my legs. In those days our ministers wore the white surplice over the black cassock. Adam would wrap himself in its folds and reverentially kiss my hand as if I were the pope or the Godfather.

We moved only twice after our country parsonage, first to another church in Virginia, and then to Durham, North Carolina, where I settled into teaching at Duke and Tracy attended law school and joined a local firm. Our kids did not grow up on the Midwestern checkerboard that would always be home to Tracy and me, but far away on the southern Piedmont where Adam would spend the rest of his life. The Midwest receded into memory as if belonging to a distant geologic age, and we all became people of the Piedmont and southerners of a sort. The first time we flew over the region, we admired its rolling emerald hills and low ridges, but when Tracy and I walked the land and eventually bought some property of our own, we discovered that it was littered with shards of blue granite, crystal, and quartz, some of it half a billion years old, all of it broken and half-exposed like neglected tombstones.

Of our two children, Sarah was the internationalist who would eventually become a political scientist and travel the world. Adam was more suited to the conventions of southern living and would make a life and legal career in his own back-yard. Even the slant and relaxed pace of the language would find a home in him, but without the ironic southern edge. When he said of an opponent, "Bless his heart," or "God love him," he almost always meant it.

He could not remember, and like most Carolinians, could not imagine, living anywhere else. He was not one to go on about the beauties of the South, but he grew to love the routines of place, especially if they involved a truck and his dogs or a run in Chapel Hill on a crisp fall morning. He had the planted quality of those who when you ask them about new ventures in other parts of the country appear a bit stymied, as if to say, "But wouldn't that mean leaving here?"

He considered himself lucky his whole life. Like the rest of his generation, he paid no attention to the self-indulgence of his 1960s parents or the cautionary tales of his Depression-era grandparents, and smoothly merged into the steady-state world of the 1980s. His formative era fell neatly between the high dramas of rebellion and the numbing commonplaces of terror. The dangerous musicians of the 1960s were safely dead, and Adam and his friends made their own music without the entitlements of rage or despair. It was a happy time. When Ronald Reagan came to Duke, Adam was about fifteen. We had great seats in the basketball stadium, just to the side of the podium. We were the son and grandson of Yellow Dog Democrats, and yet after watching our president nod his way through one inspirational anecdote after another, we left the building feeling good about our country and the era we shared.

He once told me he had lived a "charmed life." He spoke in a confidential manner, as if he knew the evidence wasn't there to support his claim. He was barely out of college with nothing on the horizon beyond a summer job grading standardized tests, wait-listed by the law schools to which he had applied, no money, unlucky in love, and still fending off the effects of a mysterious disease with which he had contended most of his life. He would not have denied the facts of his life, and he was by no means an incurable optimist. But he did have a powerful sense of *favor* that hovered over him like a small, portable rainbow, the exact purposes of which he was still working out. I remember that I didn't know how to respond, since "charmed" is not a Lutheran word and there is no right answer to such a comment anyway. Others who knew him would have readily agreed to "charming." But "charmed" was a larger claim and much more difficult to substantiate, even then.

3

We were sitting in a sweltering auditorium watching a middle-school production of *Guys and Dolls*. It was a spring evening in 1984, but summer weather had come early to North Carolina. Our Adam had been given the part of the affable hoodlum, Nicely-Nicely, a role almost certainly not created for a blond boy soprano with a southern accent. He was twelve. He stopped the show that night with "Sit Down, You're Rockin' the Boat." He wore a white fedora, a striped zoot suit, and a vaudevillian bow tie. He stood four-and-a-half feet high, not counting the hat.

I remember how carefully Tracy and I studied his performance and mapped his every move. We had been doing it for several years. By that time Adam was deep into a mysterious neurological disorder that caused him to move his head and stretch his mouth in odd and exaggerated ways. Something in his musculature was stalled or hung up, and his body was straining to find the release point. He rolled his eyes and was given to spasms and impulsive gestures. It was as if this downy boy with sparkling eyes was made of rubber bands that stretched and snapped every hour of the day. He was at peace only when he slept or sang.

I agonized over this malady and considered it a crime against his beautiful person. Little as he was, Adam wanted no part of that sort of thinking. He simply called it "my problem," as if to say, "It isn't that bad, but in any case it's my trouble and not yours." Much later, he would insist, "*Dad,* it's not *theological,* okay?" and to his mom, "It's much harder on you than it is on me." Against our misgivings, he insisted on pushing himself into sink-or-swim social situations, like theater, and then amazed us by deftly incorporating the mysterious energy of the illness into his every performance. That night in *Guys and Dolls* the very name of his character provided perfect cover for an actor with a repetitive movement disorder:

BENNY: You know Nicely-Nicely Johnson.
HARRY: Yeah. How goes it?
NICELY: Nicely, nicely, thank you.

Adam was willing to live with his problem, but his parents were determined to solve it. We have a photo of our six-year-old with his white-blond bangs butchered back to the crown of his forehead; he looks like a marine recruit who changed his mind halfway through the haircut. That was my doing because I suspected he was merely blinking back the hair from his eyes. I was wrong about that, just as we were later proved wrong by the infectious disease experts and the allergists, but only after we had gotten rid of the carpet and curtains in his room, hidden his stuffed animals, taken him off sugar and gluten, and put him on a diet of pears and rice. He tolerated it all except for the rice. I reminded him that Duke was famous for its Rice Diet. "It's for fat people," he replied glumly. We also tried prayer, a faith healer, a cocker spaniel, a set of iridescent red drums (with which he made the house tremble like a tuning fork), biofeedback, self-reproach, and despair. Nothing worked.

One night Adam suffered a violent reaction to one of his medications, and his disorder shot to a new and alarming level of agitation. He said he felt "like a puppet on a tight string." This sudden intensity threw the rest of the family into a mixed state of panic and grief. We all went to our rooms. Adam holed up with his dog and the TV. Sarah closed her door and did not come out. Tracy and I turned our bedroom into a place of strategy and collapse. Adam's symptoms kept him awake through the night, and when morning came it brought questions we had never asked before: What does this mean? What will become of him?

The next day was the Fourth of July. I remember it because on that day Tracy, Sarah, and I literally took a step back from him and observed the birth of courage in a small boy. Where did it come from? Courage is a trait easily overlooked in children, since it is bundled with other, less attractive characteristics, like stubbornness and an aptitude for saying No. You would suppose courage requires knowledge of history and the understanding of consequences, but what child of eight knows about either?

The neighborhood had been planning a children's parade

with decorated bikes, flag-draped floats, and dogs in costume. Adam and Sarah had been looking forward to it, but now Adam was feeling confused and depressed by his new and stronger symptoms. By midmorning the issue of the parade came up.

"What do you want to do, honey?" we asked. The implication being, You might want to skip it this year.

For a moment or two the action stopped in our kitchen. I can still see the three healthy ones poised in a semicircle around the one with the Problem. I can see the wheels going round in his head as he weighs his two available options.

He gave the question time to sink in, then stuck an enormous wad of bubble gum into his mouth to relieve the spasms, and announced to the room, "I'm going." Then he marched to the front door and threw it open.

"Guess who came to our class today," Adam blurted out as he walked into the house after school. His voice was piping with excitement. "Go on, guess." Before we could ask who, he said, "Gene Banks!" Banks was a basketball star at Duke whom all the little boys idolized. Adam wrote poems to and about Gene Banks.

Banks was apparently taking part in a community PR program, and as luck would have it had visited Adam's class. "Gene came at the perfect time. Nolan Baxter was making fun of me. I thought I might have to punch him—hard. Anyway, Gene was there to show us about passing and dribbling, and guess who he picked to help him? Guess!"

"Surely not you?"

"Me exactly. He picked me! And when we dribbled back and forth to each other, the whole class cheered."

"Then what happened?"

"Then he left."

"But what did Gene Banks say to the class?" I asked.

"Not that much really."

It was Adam's shining moment. We only regretted that we had not been there to witness it. It did strike us as a bit extreme that after Banks left the teacher then allowed Adam to choose the punishment for the kid who had been tormenting him, which Adam proceeded to describe in arabesque detail. He talked about little else until bedtime.

Of course, it was all a lie. None of it had happened. But we didn't figure it out until the next day, and then only by chance. Tracy and Adam were shopping at Kroger where they happened to run into Adam's teacher, Mrs. Martin.

"Yesterday must have been quite a day," Tracy said. Nothing registered in Mrs. Martin, who only smiled. "I mean with Gene Banks visiting the class and choosing Adam to help him teach the group about basketball," Tracy continued.

As they talked, Adam developed an intense interest in the frozen foods section one aisle over.

"I'm sure Adam *wishes* Gene Banks had come to class," Mrs. Martin said with enough projection to reach Adam in frozen foods. "Sometimes we want things so badly that we think they have actually happened when they have occurred only in our imagination."

Over in frozen foods Adam was turning beet red, and Tracy was beginning to sound like the kid who has just been told there's no Santa Claus and is putting two and two together on the Easter Bunny. "Then I suppose you didn't allow Adam to select the punishment for that horrible little Baxter boy. . . ."

"No, I'm afraid not," she said, as if to ask, Exactly what kind of sadist do you take me for?

Tracy, Sarah, and I couldn't help but laugh about his made-up story and its embarrassing aftermath (Adam not so much), but we also understood its more sobering conclusion. It's difficult to allow someone you love to have his own day with its minor defeats and triumphs, separate and free from your monitoring of it. Tracy and I were his air-traffic controllers, and we worked hard at it every day. We carefully plotted his day at school in order to know whose air space he would enter and when. We assumed the dead spots on our radar were limited to the school bus, playground, and the boys' bathroom. We couldn't appreciate the finer points of childhood suffering, how the pain of being different spills over accepted boundaries and creates new channels and outlets in the imagination. We underestimated the cost of difference in a child who was struggling with a physical problem, probably because he was *our* child—witty, loving, and confident—who would have never admitted that third grade was a battle he was losing.

By this time Adam was seeing the leading child psychiatrist at Duke, an elderly Freudian named John Fowler, who assured us that Adam's physical problems were merely outward symptoms of an inner conflict, which over time he and Adam would identify, work through, and resolve. He said it as matter-of-factly as a plumber describes an obstruction in a long line of pipe.

Adam appears to have been a rewarding candidate for therapy—articulate, symbolically competent, and endlessly forthcoming. He never ran out of material for his grateful therapist. He was a walking inventory of jokes, riddles, word games, stories, lies, dreams, grade-school gossip, and the ordinary stuff of childhood the analyst pans for gold. All of it he offered to his good friend "Fowler," as he called him. And when he tired of the whole business he would simply say, "Let's talk about monsters," which John Fowler assured us also had meaning.

We never saw a psychological breakthrough, however, because there was nothing to break through *to*—no "worm at the core," as William James called it, and no obstruction in the line. Most of the medical literature was pointing to a physical explanation of the disorder anyway, and suggesting a variety of medications for its treatment. When I think of the web of *theory* in which little Adam was enveloped, I shudder to remember Susan Sontag's comment about illness: "Nothing is more punitive than to give a disease a meaning."

In the meantime, the children persisted in being children. All siblings are co-conspirators against their parents, and Sarah and Adam were no exception. They charted the soft spots and vulnerabilities in each of their parents and brilliantly exploited them. Adam understood that Sarah's achievements at school created capital for them both at home. She knew we could not resist her brother's sense of humor and gift of gab. That she had plowed through *A Child's History of the World* somehow redounded to his benefit; that he could please us by reciting "Taffy was a Welshman / Taffy was a thief" worked to her advantage as well. Together, they played us.

When they were very little, I would give them each a quarter if they could find my car keys, sunglasses, or some little thing I was always misplacing. They loved the challenge, and the money made them feel rich. It was a short step from finding my car keys to *hiding* my car keys and then producing them for cash. It may have been their first conspiracy.

On rare snowy days in North Carolina, they would be waiting for me when I got home from work. One afternoon, they made snow angels and a fort in the backyard until, tiring of that, they stockpiled an arsenal of ice-balls on the picnic table. When I got out of the car, they flew around the garage in their hooded parkas like Jedi, pelting me with ice the size of baseballs. Sarah's wire-rimmed, oval glasses were totally fogged. We were laughing and screaming at the top of our lungs; I turned my ankle on the lip of the driveway and went facedown in the snow, still laughing but now screaming in pain at the same time. They took it as a ploy on my part and kept on pelting. "Daddy's not kidding," I remember pleading. "He hurts *bad!*"

On a family vacation to Nags Head, it rained one afternoon, which meant the rolling dunes of Jockey's Ridge were not available for pirate games. At a used books store in town it was Adam who first came across the copy of *Oliver Twist*. For some time I had been telling them bedtime stories from the novel without bothering with attribution. He immediately called Sarah's attention to the book by "Mr. Dickens." Together, as they flipped through the etchings of Oliver, Fagin, and the Artful Dodger, their outrage grew. It would last a lifetime.

When eight-year-old Sarah wrote her "memoirs," in cursive on loose-leaf paper bound through the holes by a ribbon, she began with the sentences, "Adam was a prince. My brother and I lived together in Fairyland. We could fly."

Together, the children drew us into their lives of relentless make-believe, and the four of us lost ourselves in other plots and characters, many of which we sustained over months and even years. The games provided a long-running commentary on our family roles and daily experiences. Tracy was the proprietor of Peggy's Restaurant. Peggy was always available and her modest restaurant was always open. I was Mister, the amiable but ineffectual schoolteacher, or sometimes Jackie Boy, the laziest and most badly behaved boy in class. Seven-year-old Sarah played a nameless, sadistic school principal who carried a club of rolled magazines. She was the law. Adam was a boy named Todd, who was easily and frequently misled by others.

One morning at breakfast, Sarah told Tracy and me she had dreamed that night of Jesus. She was twelve, and by this time we had all outgrown our games of make-believe. "Jesus!" we exclaimed. "What happened? What'd he look like?"

"I don't know, I really didn't see him. He had just gone around the corner. I could only see his back, but I called to him."

"Really?" we said. "What did you say?"

"I said, 'Hey—*Hey!*—help my brother!'"

Inevitably, the little prince grows up to become the little nuisance who gets into your things, horns in on your social life, and shatters your display of teacups with his drumming. Secretly, he worships his sister's authority, but for the usual, universal reasons he is compelled to challenge it on a daily basis. The two of them enter a season of mutual vigilance that will last intermittently through high school until the siblings rediscover one another and their paths converge again in friendship.

On April 13, 2005, the first call from his cell phone went out to her.

During his mid-teens, every dimension of the syndrome began to moderate and recede from the center toward the circumference of our lives. What finally happened turned out to be far less dramatic than our long and anguished search for meaning. We noticed that he, and we, began to speak of it retrospectively, and when as a college freshman he wrote an essay about it, he cast it in the past tense. He was never entirely free of the disorder, but then he had never made the slightest concession to it anyway. What I had considered a curse he treated as atmosphere, like weather, for which you might make the smallest of adjustments—an umbrella or a canvas jacket—but nothing more. Some of his symptoms remained, but their toll in fatigue and suffering, along with the army of punitive metaphors that traveled with them, simply moved on. It was nothing more dramatic than that: foreground slips into background; a powerful plot drifts into subplot, and no one seems to notice.

Either nothing worked—including the dog, drums, biofeedback, Fowler, and prayer—or everything worked—including the dog, drums, biofeedback, Fowler, and prayer—but in God's own time. When it is impossible to understand why something good falls into your life, Christians call it grace and say thank you. However it happened, one door in his childhood quietly closed, another opened, and something from the future made itself known. That part of him contained in his baptismal name—*Adam, human, humus*—which was all of him, had been reborn.

By his senior year in high school he was the sexy Elvis-figure in the musical *Grease*. He wore a black leather jacket and sang "Greased Lightnin'" with such a curled lip and swiveled hips that older women in the audience squealed with delight. Later that year he played the young Seymour threatened by the carnivorous plant in *Little Shop of Horrors*. By then he stood six-foot-three with sandy, swept-back hair and the legs and instincts of a dancer.

At the University of North Carolina he perfected his falsetto in the role of a man disguised as a woman in the UNC production of *Chicago* (the part of Mary Sunshine was cut from the film). He wore a little black dress and high heels for the role. His sister taught him how to walk and move his hips like a woman. His mother provided a necklace and some dangly earrings. I told him how proud it made a dad to see his boy on the stage in panty hose and pumps.

I also advised him, "It's about time you thought about how to earn a living," which even he admitted he couldn't do in the theater. "You are so right, Dad," he said—and promptly switched his major to philosophy.

Chicago was his last production before he changed majors and decided to go to law school. Somewhere between Mary Sunshine and Criminal Procedure he grew up, buckled down, fell in love, and passed the bar. But his voice never changed.

Until the day they erased it from his phone, it was a teenager's voice, as sharp and beardless as the soaring Seymour's and as full of the future as ever.

His mother seems to know him the way all mothers know their children: her body remembers his. First by its mysterious presence, then by multiple dampnesses, and finally by touch—the skinny arm tossed carelessly around her shoulder, the surprising ripples of tension across the small of his back (unexpected in one so easygoing), the delicate hands of such a big boy, the rough nub of his old Harris Tweed sport coat.

But I know him otherwise. I know him by ear, as if he were still singing to me, but from a place where words are no longer necessary or even desired—except perhaps for the occasional "Hey, *Dad*."

4

When Adam was a very little boy, he and I played one of those bedtime games that always ends in an uproar of giggling and roughhousing and succeeds only in keeping the child awake. "Why do you do that?" Tracy would ask with exasperation. But she knew.

The game was called "Whose Boy Are You?" and the whole thing consisted in my asking the question and Adam responding with the name of any man he could think of—his way of saying, "Anybody's boy but yours." He usually began with men we knew from church or the neighborhood and ended with famous men from TV or sports. One night he claimed to be the son of the sportscaster Howard Cosell.

The game was only resolved by more headlocks and uncontrolled giggling until he confessed: he was mine.

In summer we broke in our baseball gloves by soaking them for days with neatsfoot oil and wrapping them in rags.

We played "burnout" in a clearing behind the trees in our backyard, a place the children called "The Way Back." There was nothing more to the game than firing a baseball back and forth for hours on end, and then comparing palms afterward to see whose was redder and more swollen.

On winter evenings it was basketball on the driveway beneath the security lights mounted above the garage. We played the game as a contact sport with a lot of hacking, shoving, and trash-talking, neither of us willing to call it a night. Until Tracy, insisting from the kitchen door: "Rick and Adam, do you want to eat or not? *Boys!*"

After he grew eight inches in the summer of his fifteenth year, we turned our attention from basketball to tennis. One morning when I came down to breakfast, I found a note from him on the kitchen table. It had always been his way to leave written messages for us around the house. Scratched in his usual backslant, this one riffed on one of his heroes, Muhammad Ali:

> *I hit like Jimmy,*
> *Dive like Becker.*
> *Your backhand sucks,*
> *Mine is better.*
> *Comebacks like Lendl,*
> *The Passion of Borg,*
> *Play with me*
> *And visit the morgue!*

Tracy and Adam did not have to play games like "Whose Boy Are You?" because mothers and sons know the answer to that one. She can put her arms around her little boy, no matter how big, surly, and unshaven, and say, "I love you, Sweetie," and he will respond in kind without a hint of embarrassment. She isn't saddled with the male habit of indirection by which love may only be mediated by a thrown ball, a fishing trip, or scuffling while half hugging on the driveway.

When he went away to college, he started taking courses in drama and philosophy and stopped going to church every Sunday. He also befriended homeless people on East Franklin Street in Chapel Hill, learned their names, and went with them to AA meetings at the Methodist church. In effect, he switched from a Sunday morning believer to a Tuesday night seeker who was finding more answers in the church basement than in the sanctuary.

In those years, Adam and I took our competition up a notch from basketball and tennis to religion. He posed the usual questions that perplex all believers but only sophomores are allowed to ask out loud. He peppered his speeches with what he had learned in philosophy class that morning. I stocked my rebuttals with what I could remember from seminary twenty-five years earlier. He wanted to know how Christians can accept the Bible's worldview in the age of science, and I answered that there are orders of truth, and some are higher than others. Whereupon he accused me of "fideism," which I had to look up later that evening: "the theory that belief or revelation is superior to reason as a source of truth."

I remember another session at the Carolina Coffee Shop

near campus. We were in his regular booth at the back of the restaurant, where he often studied and one of the waitresses would sit with him and help him with his symbolic logic. He asked me, "Why do you pray when God already knows everything you need?"

I replied, "What's this *you* business?"

He looked a little chagrined but did not say "we." "We" would have softened the question and ruined the debate. "Why do *Christians* pray when God already knows everything *they* need?"

"Every creature needs to respond to God, but human beings most of all. It's our special privilege given to us at creation," I said, wishing that just once I could talk to my son about religion without sounding like a professor.

He asked me why God allows some people to suffer but not others, and I replied that I didn't know. He asked his questions respectfully, as a believer, but a believer who has taken a holiday from dogma, tradition, and the authority of his father.

Already when he was in high school we had had our little differences over church attendance. Nothing major. In fact, sometimes we skipped out together and went to a nearby bakery on Ninth Street. One Sunday morning, however, I said to him, "I want to see you in church today." I was scheduled to preach in Duke Chapel, which was always a big deal to me. He had other plans, but I insisted. Later that morning, when I climbed into the pulpit, I looked down to see him sitting with Tracy and Sarah in the fifth or sixth row. He seemed genuinely pleased to be in church and shot me an encouraging, uncomplicated smile. Everything was perfect except for his outfit. He was wearing my pants, my belt, my shirt, one of my ties, my sport coat, and (I later discovered) my shoes and socks. It was teenaged performance art of the highest caliber. I took it to be his way of saying, *You want another you? Okay, you've got him.*

A young man like Adam leaves home with what he has learned against his will in Sunday school, confirmation class, and acolyte training. In college he faces a fusillade of objections from Hume, Kant, Marx, and Rousseau, whose names rarely come up in confirmation class or the Sunday sermon. The gifts that actually formed and nurtured him—community, sacraments, liturgy, and friendship—don't count as knowledge on Tuesday and Thursday mornings in the Philosophy of Religion. When I referred to our common life of faith as itself a source of knowledge, he replied almost pityingly, like a child who has noticed that the old man has begun to lose it, "But *Dad,* that's not an argument." This always pleased me because I wanted him to use academic words like "argument" and "fideism," wanted him to be at home with Hume and Kant, and I wanted him to best me in every contest, even this one.

During his third year in college, Adam played drums in a rock band, got an earring and a buzz-cut, acquired a twice-wrecked BMW, earned a black belt in Tae Kwon Do, taught a self-defense class for women, and wrote a detective novel—all when he wasn't "busy studying."

The training hall became a way of life for him. Tae Kwon Do mirrors the unity of mind and body by means of meditation and the choreography of Olympic-style sparring. Adam called it "fighting," as in "I have a big fight this weekend." Tae Kwon Do also provides an arena in which fear is allowed to be present and the student is permitted to fail. Using his lean frame and height advantage, he won the North Carolina Open by beating the best red belt in the state. Later he fought and lost a credible fight against a future Olympic medalist. It seemed to me that he courted the fear of fighting as much as the fight itself: both were something to be endured and overcome. In one of his many letters he wrote, "I have a tourney coming up Saturday in Raleigh. I am trying not to care whether I win or lose, as long as I do my best. So far—this is NOT WORKING AT ALL."

By the time he got his black belt, he could do a hundred push-ups, endless sit-ups, and run the stairs of his apartment building for hours. With his new haircut and washboard abs, he might have been a skinhead or a leatherneck. He sent us funny, staged photos of himself purportedly studying, a stack of books arranged in the background, but he was clearly misplaced in a library. But for now, his letters seemed to say, my element is the fight.

When he did sit down to study, he was often distracted by his novel, a murder mystery set in Chapel Hill. It begins with this sentence: "It was almost ten thirty a.m. as he sat on the edge of his bed, staring at his boots and wishing he had gotten more sleep." Its main character exhales "blue pencils of smoke" from his Viceroy cigarette, and so on.

The novel was fine. Even the fighting was fine. It was the rock band that was the problem.

Adam was sharing an off-campus apartment with the leader of the band, a drug-dabbling introvert named Jeff. He was susceptible to mellow types like Jeff, who call you "man" and share your taste in Nirvana and Pearl Jam and can't be bothered with details.

"I want you to have friends, Adam. I think everybody needs friends," I said. "God knows, there must be twenty-five thousand options in Chapel Hill, but is *this* one capable of being a true friend to you?"

"What you really mean is, 'Is this guy a Dukie? Is he a preppie?' You are not the only one who has a deep under-standing of *people*. I think I know people, too. Friends mean a lot to me. You have 'colleagues,' I have friends. *Please,* don't tell me you choose your friends by going down a list of values and checking them off. My friends want to be with me. That's what it's all about."

This was a conversation we had at the dumpster near his apartment. It was a neutral location where we met on a regular basis to talk. Sometimes I delivered cookies from his mother or made cash drops, like a bagman.

A few months later, we had another conversation in which each of us adopted a very different, less combative tone. He called me at my office.

"Hey, *Dad.*"

"Yeah, man."

"I can't do this anymore."

"*Jeff.*"

"Right. I can't keep up with this guy. He's into drugs, and he has dopeheads in the apartment. The place is a wreck from last night. It's the last straw. I can't live like this. I just can't."

I said, "What if I showed up tomorrow morning with a U-Haul, say, eight-thirty? Would that be okay? Is a truck okay? We can put you up at home and figure out the next step from there. What do you think?"

He didn't hesitate to reply, "I'll be waiting for you tomorrow at eight-thirty."

And he was. Standing in the doorway, peering down the stairway toward the parking lot with a resolute look on his face. He was wearing a Carolina sweatshirt and a pair of faded jeans. Behind the open door, the apartment was strewn with bottles and junk. A floor lamp was splayed across a coffee table; the beds were covered with clothes and open suitcases.

I had never seen Adam so upset. "I *told* him you were coming," he said, as if he simply could not comprehend why anyone wouldn't spruce up the place for his roommate's dad. He nearly ground his teeth as he said it.

We had the truck loaded by ten o'clock and by ten-thirty we were out of there, sitting in a diner on the bypass between Chapel Hill and Durham, devouring a breakfast of pancakes, bacon, eggs, grits, and coffee. The stress and urgency of the move had lifted, and it was simply Saturday morning, and Saturday's feast was steaming between us. We shared it in a narrow booth with our elbows on the table and our knees practically touching.

That day it felt as if an old game, or series of games, had finally come to an end. He stayed with Tracy and me for the rest of the spring term until he found his own apartment and returned for his senior year. We lived together as friends.

By this time Sarah was about to graduate from Georgetown and begin a one-year internship in South Africa, where, during the last dangerous days of apartheid, she would teach in a Catholic school in a homeland north of Pietersburg. She

would live in a low wooden building bordered by purple jac-
aranda and the graves of priests and nuns. She would travel
alone in the country on crowded buses and wait in the cities at
the notorious taxi stands.

Our children were finished with splashing in the tidal
pools of Nags Head, making snow angels in the backyard, and
pretending to be other, more interesting children. They were
finished with being children altogether, and we were feeling finished with our job of launching and protecting them.
They would each go away, one to be challenged and molded
in Africa, another to find his bearings eight miles from home
in Chapel Hill.

The Labyrinth

5

On April 13, 2005, I stood at a cylindrical wall of glass on the top floor of the medical center's main tower and, one by one, took inventory of the people I loved. This is what you do when you are under siege. You find a secure place in the fortress with a commanding view of the enemy and make a list of the people you must defend at all costs. You assign places to them on the battlements and coordinate their movements like a commanding officer, even though you are not in command. From where I stood in the tower I could see other towers and pyramids of glass, stacked cubes of research buildings in the distance, and on a nearby rooftop a helipad with a translucent blue copter standing by. I felt as if the area had been secured and the people I loved were protected.

Tracy and I were tracking every member of our immediate family, three of whom were in the hospital that day. I was in the ER with her father Bob who had suffered a heart arrhythmia early that morning. Tracy was on the seventh floor with her mother Nina who was being treated for uterine cancer.

Two hundred miles to the north, our daughter Sarah was about to board a plane from Charlottesville, Virginia, to New Haven, where she was to make a presentation in a graduate seminar at Yale. Twenty miles to the east of us, inside a doublewide with an old couch on the porch and chickens out front, Adam's wife, Jenny, was practicing her craft of occupational therapy, teaching a stroke victim how to make breakfast for herself.

And inside Jenny, in a place of nourishment and peace, an unnamed baby girl had found the safest chamber of all.

Adam was in an adjoining clinic moving from station to station on one of his usual three-month checkups for mysterious shadows, nodes, masses, and other signs of "metastatic activity." He would have been plying the technician with questions about the design of the scanner and half joking about the lethality of the process.

Sixteen months earlier a surgeon had taken a melanoma from Adam's back. He got it all, he said. Even the sentinel lymph nodes were free of cancer. We wept for joy. Still, the lesion was deep and the cells were "angry," he said.

He was sent home with an ugly scar and a 30 percent chance of recurrence. Which is to say, if God produced ten Adams with his identical lesion-depth, histological makeup, and family history, seven of the ten would walk away. For the unlucky three, a recurrence would be "difficult to treat," the surgeon said with unmistakable finality. That's three crashes for every ten takeoffs, three Katrinas for every ten hurricanes.

We were told these were very good odds and we should be grateful for them.

Who are *these oddsmakers?* I thought. Like Job, I would like to meet them and make my arguments before them.

I remember assuring Tracy, "They won't lose him." By "they," I must have meant the oddsmakers themselves: the pyramids of steel and glass, the crisp lab coats, the surgeon's reputation, the blue copter, the sheer ascendant force of this powerful enterprise. I felt we had cleared security, taken our places, and were buckled in. Competent pilots were checking their instruments. We were safe in the mother ship and safer still in the cocoon of love and accomplishment our family had fashioned for itself.

Then my cell phone rang.

When I answered it, I bolted from Bob's room without a word of explanation. I began running, the way looters and cowards run, away from the police or whatever it is they are afraid of, lost in the sheer abandonment of running. I ran along a broad corridor away from the secure zone of the ER and into the outer membrane of the main lobby of the hospital. From there I fast-walked my way into a narrower, more congested hallway and a confusing warren of smaller rooms. I had gotten badly turned around in a building I'd known for twenty years.

Calling Tracy as I ran, I repeated Adam's message. Without a word, she cried into my ear, and I could hear the commotion as she too bolted through the door of her mother's room into her own chaos. "Mama, I have to go," I heard her say. "It's Adam."

For a second time I circled the lobby, passed the gift shop, and stupidly made a wrong turn through doors marked DO NOT ENTER. I found myself at the checkpoint in the ER again, where I didn't want to be and where I had to remove my watch, coins, and keys and pass through a screening device. Of course, Adam was nowhere near the ER—he was in an adjacent building. I was no nearer to Adam than when I'd begun. In the ER I ran past intake rooms with strangers leaning vacantly in doorways, waiting for something to happen or for someone to come. They didn't change expression as they watched me fly by. No one said, "Sir, are you lost? Where are you trying to be? Does this building seem strange to you?" My heart was thumping. I charged out of the emergency suite a second time and kept running until I completed a vast and futile circuit, found the elevator in the lobby, and took it down to the rail level for transport to the clinics.

By some miracle Tracy and I met on the crowded platform. I think she had been running too. She was clammy and winded like me. We held each other for a minute or so while strangers streamed by us. Then we boarded the tram together and set out to find our son.

We found him where he said he would be, in a consulting room in 2 K with his oncologist and a younger resident named Tim. The room was as white and strange as all the others. The light was blinding.

We entered with the oncologist's speech in progress. We

said practically nothing to Adam because the doctor was talking: "Metastatic melanoma typically does not respond well to radiation or chemotherapy," he said, and went on to give the reasons why this would be a difficult course of treatments. We listened in silence.

The oncologist was an unflappable man with a cherubic face and a perfect wave of sandy hair across his forehead. He had been following Adam's progress for sixteen months. I couldn't help but admire the rationality with which he laid out the problem. He spoke in perfectly constructed sentences with no syntactical breaks or interjections, as if he had diagrammed them before our meeting. Every word was a blade with which he cleanly slashed treatment options and favorable outcomes. *He's done this before,* I thought, *and at what emotional cost to himself as well.* On the Big Board, the numbers were spinning and Adam's "very good odds" were changing as the oncologist spoke. Invert a few percentages and deftly substitute "response to therapy" in place of "non-recurrence" of the cancer, and the deed is done. I could feel the future falling away.

We were plunging from a Stage 2 with a 70 percent chance of non-recurrence to a Stage 4 with a 15 percent chance of *response to treatment*—no matter how minimal or pitifully temporary—with absolutely no talk of cure, no Stage 5, no reasonable prospects for effective treatment, and no mention of survival. And it was happening in real time with no opportunity for us to slow the pace of this lecture. *I wonder how they rehearse scenes like this in medical school,* I thought. *Or do they?*

At this point, we would have welcomed the human touch—some crumb of acknowledgment that, even though he was the doctor and our son was the patient, we were at least capable, all of us, of a common sorrow, no matter how differently it might be expressed. But then perhaps it was unfair to expect a professional to summon *any* emotion comparable to what we were feeling. Did we really need the oncologist's tears to get us through this meeting? Or was there a mercy in these uninflected sentences? Perhaps he knew we were less likely to collapse under an evenly distributed weight. *What did you want,* I later asked myself, *a clinical assessment or a biblical lament?*

I wanted a lament. Instead of nodding thoughtfully, I wanted to kneel on the tile floor and bang my head on something metal. I wanted to crush Adam's head to my chest and kiss him as I did when he was five. I wanted to pull him back into the old place of safety, as it used to be when he was hurt or afraid, when there *was* such a place.

To my question about surgery the oncologist was quickly and firmly dismissive. It was clear Adam had too many sites. Apparently, this had been discussed before Tracy and I arrived.

"We would like to enroll you in a clinical trial that doesn't begin until the end of next week," the oncologist said. The treatment of metastatic melanoma is a palliative intervention, but clinical trials are important and this one would be "worth waiting for." He told us about a new drug called Proleukin that helps the immune system fight off infections. Some patients have responded beautifully to this therapy. "As always," the oncologist continued, "you would benefit from the enhanced monitoring that comes with a larger study." Vigorous nodding from Tim's side of the room.

Then, as if to anticipate the patient's attempt to probe the doctor's heart, the oncologist added, "If it were a member of my family, I would do the clinical trial." He didn't say "my son" or "my daughter." He kept it generic.

There is a rhetoric that greases these skids. It is the rhetoric of managed defeat. It whittles hope down to size by means of a rational sequence of failures until the slim promontory on which the patient stands crumbles and the patient disappears. Standard treatments give way to newer therapies (no longer called treatments), which spawn innovative therapies, from which is selected the latest or most dangerous therapy, the failure of which necessitates an experimental drug whose only name is a government number. Eventually, the rhetoric shifts from quantifiable results, which, you must understand, vary from tumor to tumor, to the elusive "quality of life," which has already been ruined by the treatments themselves.

Adam was reclining on an examination table against the wall, listening. He was lying on his side, propped up on one elbow, with his right cheek and jaw resting in his palm. He was wearing gray slacks and a soft white shirt with the sleeves rolled up. His hair fell over his fingers, and his legs dangled beyond the edge of the table. I thought, *Man, do you look great,* a parental tic dating no doubt from a time when I was sure he would never again wear anything but cutoffs and sweatshirts with butchered sleeves. It was also my way of hitting back at the smooth-talking oncologist and the cancer itself. He looks *great.*

Adam had hardly spoken since we entered the room. At the mention of the clinical trial he laughed, as did we all for the first and only time that day. It was a quickie, heard-this-one-before laugh, because only sixteen months earlier we *had* heard it before—about a clinical trial with interferon, the immunotherapy that enhances the body's ability to fight off cancer. Adam had done the course of experimental treatments after his original surgery and tolerated the standard side effects of nausea and fatigue. In the run-up to the trial he was not informed that an earlier study had shown that those treated with interferon enjoy a relatively longer period of remission from the melanoma—but live not one day longer.

When he completed the interferon therapy, he went back to his job as an assistant district attorney in eastern Carolina. His brush with cancer was just that—a brush, not a blot on the rest of his life—a temporary tension that would ease with time and eventually disappear. Cancer: what an experience *that* had been.

After about twenty seconds, Adam said resolutely, "I'll take the trial." The words were no sooner out of his mouth when the oncologist moved to a final disclaimer, the way a banker discloses at the very end of the application process why you may not get the loan after all. "There is one possible dis-qualifying factor. If you have lesions in the brain, you won't be permitted to participate in the clinical trial. But we won't know that until late tomorrow."

Late in the afternoon of April 13, 2005, as the three of us left oncology and made our way through the building, our metaphors were changing. So, it was not a brush after all, but something more. It was a worm. What we had taken to be a temporary unpleasantness had now burrowed deep into the family pulp and was gnawing us from the inside out. We thought the first surgery had slaughtered it, but it has this amazing will to live, the worm does, and now it was back and eating again.

I can only guess that Adam and Jenny had known all along that it had never left. That's why they began trying to get pregnant as soon as the interferon cleared his system. They gave us their big news one evening after supper as we were loading the dishwasher: "When is Sarah due?" he asked casually about his sister's pregnancy. "January," we said. "Oh," he replied nonchalantly, "Jenny's not due till July." After which, pandemonium in our kitchen and the four of us laughing, crying, and embracing one another. In sixteen short months he had left his job in eastern North Carolina and joined Tracy's law firm in Durham. He and Jenny had bought a house, planted trees, made a baby, and set their faces toward the future, all of it in defiance of death. No wonder the worm was angry.

After our meeting with the oncologist, Adam asked Tracy and me to drive home with him and keep him company until Jenny got home from work. Clearly, he did not want to be alone. We said very little on our way to the parking deck. Tracy drove his Yukon and I sat in the back. I couldn't see his face when he finally spoke.

His first words were "Promise you will take care of my little girl," and his voice cracked, then quickly recovered. You promise me, he said, as if he were already a spirit speaking to us from beyond the grave.

By the time we had pulled onto his street and turned into his driveway, he was still talking about the baby. She would need a family around her to love and support her. Of course, she would go to college. He already knew her intimately and understood what was best for her. It was as if he had taken a terrible blow to the head, but it had granted him mystical powers to see his unborn daughter at every stage of her life.

We made our promises in the truck, and when we were finished we went inside.

Adam and Jenny lived in a small but spectacular tree house, all planes and angles with lots of glass, open spaces, and a tiny observation deck above their bedroom at the very top. The entry hall opened downward via two broad steps into a high-ceilinged, Pottery Barn living room with dog-worn hardwood floors and an elevated iron stove. One open-tread stairway led down to a TV room and study; another went up to the master bedroom, which was the crown of the house and their hideaway in the trees. Its ceiling was low and, despite Adam's height, the bed was a standard double. Only people who doted on each other's bodies would have chosen a bedroom and a bed that small.

As we walked into the house we were uproariously greeted by Sadie, a golden retriever, and Winston, an arthritic, 160-pound Great Dane. Adam talked his usual high-pitched baby talk to his dogs and rolled around on the floor with them for a bit until they ate their snacks, got bored, and fell asleep at his feet. Then the three of us sat quietly on the couch like strangers at a bus stop and waited for Jenny to come home.

The house had become a museum overnight. Its rooms might have been preserved as exhibits of an ordinary domestic scene just as it was before the volcano blew. A bowl of fruit was posed on the dining room table in the late afternoon light. An open box of Wheat Thins on the counter in the kitchen. The fridge papered with notes and messages that would never again matter. The air had never been so heavy in these rooms;

it made us lethargic and added to the weight of our silence. We were there, but the house was empty.

Tracy and I felt awkward and out of place. It's not the parents who should be entering their children's living space, glancing at yesterday's mail, and noticing the dishes in the sink. It's not the old folks who should be moving with purpose, while the youngster sinks into the couch with a sigh. Once Dad has had his stroke or Mom is finally gone, it's the children's duty to do a last walk-through and sort out their things. Tracy and I had already gotten it backward. It's the children's job, not the parents', to find the hidden key and enter the empty house.

My heart ached when I saw Jenny walking across the driveway toward the porch. She is tall and beautiful with delicate features and a quiet manner. When she is happy she shows it by blushing; when she is sad she simply turns pale. Did she wonder what her in-laws were doing in her living room at five in the afternoon? Adam went outside and met her on the porch with his news. In about five minutes they came in. They were holding hands, but Jenny seemed alone in a way I had never seen before. Her face was white. In a matter of minutes she had crossed over from one country and joined her husband in another.

The next day we learned the melanoma was indeed in Adam's brain. He had four separate, inoperable lesions. Forget the Proleukin for the time being. That was yesterday. Forget treating the body altogether, the oncologist seemed to say. If we can't stop it in the brain, who cares what happens in the body?

Tracy and I were each on a telephone in our bedroom

talking to the doctor. In an effort to reduce the lesions in the brain, they would start Adam on whole-brain radiation and standard chemotherapy at the same time. If these therapies held the tumors at bay or shrank them, stereotactic, or pinpoint radiation was a possibility down the line. The oncologist offered these options with matter-of-fact professionalism, as if he had not said the day before that they almost never work.

"If the radiation doesn't reduce the lesions in the brain, how long does Adam have to live?" I asked.

"Adam prefers not to quantify his situation," he said, "and one really can't predict."

"We understand," Tracy and I said in unison. He knew that Adam didn't want to hear a number. We both appreciated the oncologist's deference to Adam's wishes.

"But if you had to pre—"

"Six months."

"The baby is due in about three months," we said, as if the comment were self-explanatory. We drew the universally approved inference that the merest sighting of this child would offset the tragedy and prove redemptive for us all.

"Six months seems about right," he said.

6

That very night I dreamed that a doe had broken into the small stone pool behind our house and was trapped in it. It was too tired to struggle, and only its nose and terrified eyes bobbed silently above the surface. Soon it would drown. Where was its mother? How had it gotten through the fence made of wood and steel cables? And once in the pool, could it be saved?

From the day of Adam's telephone call to me, I began dreaming in a way I had never dreamed before. It was no longer safe to fall asleep at night, and waking up in the morning wasn't much better. The dreams came in rude splashes of color, in orange and purple and yellow. But the dawn was always gray and weighted with liminal suggestions of dread.

One night I had a dream about a dream. In it, Adam's diagnosis was only a dream and nothing more. I dreamed that another world had been revealed to me in a dream. It was a

world in which Adam did not have cancer and was not terminally ill. The trick was to get from this dream to the other
one and to find a way to the better world. But it existed on
the other side of a large steel door that was not only locked
but bolted and bordered with rivets. Why, I wondered in my
dream, *why* should there even *be* such a door that leads to happiness if it can't be opened? Of course, it was a relief to know
that there was a place of safety in which he was not really
dying, but, try as I might, I couldn't open the steel door. And
in my dream, I could not wake up from my dream.

Then the doorbell rang. I answered it to find the CEO of Duke
Hospital standing at the side entrance to our house. I was
surprised that such an important person would come to the
laundry room door. What's going on? I asked. He was shifting
from foot to foot, looking very serious with a sheaf of papers
in his hand. At his side stood the president of the university,
his hands clasped across his midriff as if in prayer. *My God,* I
thought, *what has happened?* They were flanked by two other
doctors, including the head of oncology. A couple of university lawyers with briefcases were positioned just behind them.

Before I could say, "Why are you here?" the CEO
addressed me in a voice that was both grave and unmistakably
relieved. "There has been a terrible mistake," he stammered,
"a miscarriage of medical care. I don't know how to begin,
except to say, Adam does not have cancer."

He went on to explain that the surgeon who operated on
Adam is apparently a psychopath who falsified the lab reports

on the tumors he removed in order to enhance his reputation. Adam never had cancer. He has been put through these various treatments for nothing. The lawyers apparently came along because no one knew if we would be angry or pleased. I was stunned, then overjoyed. A bottle of champagne materialized, and right there in our laundry room we drank a toast to Adam's health.

In other versions of this dream it is the lab technician who is the villain, living to inflict misery on people she doesn't know. In yet another version, the psychopath is the radiologist who had it in for Adam and has consistently falsified his findings. There are no tumors or lesions, and there never were.

I considered the Dream of the Mistake my flagship dream. It was so realistic and satisfying that it quickly evolved into a successful and long-running daydream. Whenever it rolled in, it took me away and cleanly separated me from whatever I was doing. If I was at the computer, I stared at the screen as if watching a movie of my dream. If I was driving, I was lucky not to run off the road.

So it would go for the duration of Adam's illness: nothing less than a cavalcade of dreams, fantasies, and reveries—medical science by day, sheer Kafka by night. What must be contained at all costs in the light of day will run rampant at the midnight hour. Fear is suppressible, terror is not.

A friend of mine on our faculty put me in touch with *her* good friend in Alexandria, Virginia, whose husband offered to put me in touch with *his* colleague at the National Institutes of

Health who was doing exciting research on the immune system's response to metastatic melanoma. I thought of the film *Six Degrees of Separation* and quickly bought the concept.

I got hold of the man's home phone number and shamelessly called him away from a dinner party to talk to him about a young man he had never met. He spoke to me with unbelievable kindness as if he understood and personally identified with all my fears. This wonderful man explained immunotherapy in detail and gave me the names of other leading researchers, some of whom he was sure would be willing to accept patients with lesions in the brain. I had hit a gold mine of hope.

While he attended to his law practice, Adam gave me the go-ahead to investigate additional forms of treatment. I came across the Musella Foundation *Brain Tumor Guide for the Newly Diagnosed* on the Internet; it advised aggressiveness in research: "Understanding current availability of clinical trials requires time and due diligence, something many physicians lack. You must search out the appropriate trials available for your specific tumor-type, always advocating in your own best interest towards a cure."

A little due diligence confirmed and expanded everything the NIH doctor had explained to me. The Internet makes it possible to shop for treatments the way one searches for the best hotel buys or the cheapest airline tickets. It is not difficult to hook up with a hospital representative online, to indicate one's preference for a specific doctor or treatment, to jet down, say, to Houston, and to be streamed into the assessment system of a major cancer center, all inside a week's time. At MD Anderson, for example, seventeen separate melanoma trials were under way and available. How to market such complexity? One treatment center tried to simplify the immune system by means of a ridiculous analogy to an Alfred Hitchcock movie, *Sabotage,* in which a terrorist attempts to shut down London's electrical system. The ad continued, "Change the setting from London to the microscopic world of living tissue, replace the actors with human cells, and the film could be an allegory for the drama that takes place between cancer cells and the immune system." Adam's doctor had no objection to our research, but he knew our problem wasn't the confusing array of treatment options: he had seen the scans.

These desperate phone calls and Web searches must have stimulated another of my dreams, one of my favorites. It was about a father-son outing to a baseball game and an advanced cancer-research center. In my dream, Adam is admitted for treatment to a branch of NIH that, serendipitously, is located a couple of blocks from Yankee Stadium in the Bronx. The treatments are so mild that he feels well enough for us to have dinner and attend several games. We have a solid time. We eat hot dogs and share bags of popcorn, and I explain the finer points of the game to him. There is some suffering to be sure, but it is nothing the two of us can't handle. Adam is miraculously/scientifically restored (who cares how?), and we return to North Carolina in triumph. The rest of the family meets us at the airport, and we stage a noisy celebration right there in the terminal. Again, there is champagne.

Within a few days of our inquiries, every cancer center we contacted rejected Adam as a suitable candidate for therapeutic trials. Overnight he had become the deserving student who through no fault of his own is turned down by every college to which he applies. NIH would accept him only if the radiation stabilized his brain lesions or reduced them, and that could not be determined for several months. There would be no treatments at a fictional research center, no male bonding in the Big Apple, and no champagne. Our trip to Yankee Stadium was off.

At his rejection by NIH, Adam appeared to shift into executive mode and disengage from his treatments. "It makes perfect sense," he said, adding with uncharacteristic formality, "Thanks for your efforts, Dad." His demeanor was that of the losing candidate who is determined to take the high road, no matter how bitter the loss. Earlier, he had been more candid with his mother. As soon as he found out about "the brain" he admitted to her, "It's a relief, really. No last-minute maneuvers, no impossible choices, no surprises ahead. Weird to say, it's a relief to know what I'm up against."

7

A few days before these crushing disappointments, Adam was the subject of a spectacular and well-publicized success. It was a murder trial.

In the fall of 2004 a young man named Bo Dye had killed an acquaintance with a paring knife in a housing project in East Durham. Dye claimed the other man was high on drugs and had attacked him without provocation. This much was clear: the two had struggled with the knife on a busy street corner in plain view of a circle of spectators, including a policeman in a nearby squad car, who inexplicably looked on without intervening. The case would not only put Dye on trial, but the Durham Police Department as well. Dye pled self-defense, and Adam, who was the same age as Bo Dye and, like Dye, had a baby on the way, defended him. The trial was scheduled for mid-March 2005.

By this time Adam was a member of Tracy's law firm in

Durham. The two of them had fantasized about practicing together for a long time, and now, with five years of public service law and a brush with cancer behind him, it was time. He had given up his job as assistant district attorney in Wilson, North Carolina, in the eastern part of the state, and he and Jenny had moved to Durham. He said to me, "Mom has a lot to teach me, and I don't know how long she plans to practice," as if Tracy were the one who might be short on time. He joined her firm on the condition that he be allowed to work evenings and weekends for the Office of the Capital Defender in Durham. He was one of a handful of lawyers qualified by the state to defend against the death penalty. Bo Dye was his first capital case.

In his opposition to the death penalty Adam was responding to something basic in his own makeup, a streak of moral outrage that had been there since he was a kid. He would later add legal and religious reasoning to his convictions, but the convictions themselves originated elsewhere. As a boy he read and obsessively reread exactly three books: *The Chronicles of Narnia, The Catcher in the Rye,* and *To Kill a Mockingbird. Narnia* opened his eyes to the supernatural in ways that Sunday school never did (when I explained the Christ symbolism of the series, he replied, "Well, *that* ruins it"). Holden Caulfield in *Catcher in the Rye* taught him to spot a phony a mile away and to maintain a healthy suspicion of well-adjusted people. Like Holden, he would have gladly erased every "fuck you" from the schoolhouse walls of the world. But it was Atticus Finch who changed his life. He spoke reverentially of "Atticus" as if he were a trusted friend or a member of our family. When Atticus declares, "I can't live one way in town and another way in my home," Adam was taking notes.

It was Adam's way to keep us current on what he was thinking, who he was admiring, and to what he was aspiring. He was never much for small talk with his parents, but he often engaged us in what Tracy and I called "vocational conversations." These were marathon exercises in which we worked through an intractable problem, rounded something rough into shape, or brought something blurry (like his future) into focus. Each conversation was a trolley headed to the same terminal: What shall I make of my life? What's the point of making money? Do I have a future in philosophy/politics/theater? What kind of girl shall I marry? What is the ideal number of children? Three? Four? We have friends who complain that their sons never open up to them; Adam was a shop that never closed.

One evening, when Tracy and I were watching TV in the family room, he entered quietly, respectfully turned down the sound (without asking), and told us that he had decided what he was going to do with the rest of his life. He was going to "practice law." After an assortment of false starts, roommates, and girlfriends, he seemed genuinely grateful to have been shown the way forward. He didn't ask, "What do you think about me applying to a few law schools?" but he spoke of his "practice" as if he had already passed the bar and hung out his shingle. He told his mom he wanted to be an honorable southern lawyer.

He got into law school at American University and in the fall of 1995 moved to Washington, D.C. He was lonely in

Washington and thoroughly intimidated by the city, which he noticed was a hell of a lot bigger than Chapel Hill and, as he put it in a letter, "lacking in southern hospitality." He was drawn to the large public spaces and events that made him feel even smaller and more alone by comparison, like the monuments and museums and the Million Man March that took place early in his first semester. In the late afternoons he ran the path along the C & O Canal from Rock Creek Park toward M Street and back again. On weekends he roamed with the crowds in Georgetown or went to the movies by himself at the cavernous old Avalon on Connecticut Avenue. On Sundays he slipped into the equally cavernous Metropolitan Methodist Church not far from the university.

He hadn't been gone long when his first letter arrived. When others his age were discovering e-mail, he had continued to write letters, even when he lived nearby in Chapel Hill. This one was a three-page, single-spaced story about a young man writing a letter to his father; in reality, it was a clever confession of homesickness: "Reluctantly, he decided to write his father [to whom he refers elsewhere as "a kindly gentleman"] updating him on his hectic life since moving out of the nest." It ends, "He did, however, remember to mention to his father that he would be home Thanksgiving weekend, as he misses his friends, his cat, his mother's dog, and (he didn't mention this) his folks."

Adam solved the problem of loneliness by finding a place to live next door to American University at a Methodist seminary. He took his meals in the school's dining hall where he became acquainted with seminarians and faculty members. Soon he was hosting theological bull sessions in his apartment.

With his new friends, he became active in a smaller and more congenial Methodist congregation across the Key Bridge in Arlington, and there he found a home. He got involved with the young adult group in the church and came under the influence of its dynamic pastor, an open, big-hearted evangelical with a PhD in theology. Two weekends a month Adam lived in a homeless shelter near campus, where he volunteered as a cook and a bouncer. He found time to write work-study briefs against capital punishment for one of his professors and to take part in the Christian Legal Society. He also dated Methodist girls from the seminary and taught them to dance. Things were looking up.

Tracy and I made several trips to D.C. mainly to haul supplies and help with housekeeping matters. By the time I came alone to visit Adam, he was thoroughly comfortable in the city. We enjoyed a marathon Saturday that included a walk through the university, a trip to the Freer for a kimono exhibit, a Bullets game, and the late-late performance of the Capitol Steps at the Kennedy Center—all in one fabulous day. On Sunday he took me to church in Arlington, where I met his pastor and some of his friends. We came back by way of Georgetown for a late lunch at our family's favorite D.C. restaurant, Au Pied de Cochon, at the very corner where Adam as a teenager had once come within an ace of buying a "Rolex" from a guy with a suitcase. That afternoon I helped him wax his car. All weekend I took pictures of him as if he were a tourist attraction.

Adam's three years of law school came to a boisterous end at a long, teeming table in a restaurant on the Potomac, where with the whole family and a few old friends we told stories half the night and drank loud toasts to the nation's newest and brightest lawyer. Our careful Lutheran family had never celebrated the way we did that night. It was our Big Fat Graduation Party. In less than seven years, every single person at that feast would return to our dining room table in North Carolina to make a more solemn communion.

After graduation Adam clerked on the North Carolina Court of Appeals (where his mother had clerked), failed the bar exam, passed the bar exam, and then won a prestigious fellowship as a legal advocate for underrepresented people in eastern Carolina. Once a week he drove the flat road from Wilson to Goldsboro, one of several *Last Picture Show* towns in the region plagued by failing textile production and disappearing tobacco markets. There he would sit at a card table in the lobby of a public housing complex, talk to poor people about their legal problems, and try to solve them.

When his fellowship expired he took a job in Wilson as an assistant district attorney. Adam got his start in Criminal District Court, which was housed in the finest building in town, a movie-set courthouse with Doric columns and broad marble steps. Inside it was a gloomy place with fraying carpet, peeling paint, and dark paneling in the courtrooms. In district court the cases came in endless waves of breaking and entering, drunkenness and fighting, most of them incubated in the shanties and doublewides of eastern Carolina. The courthouses of small cities in the region, venues in which Adam regularly "ran" court, overflowed with rows of chained prisoners in orange jumpsuits, along with victims, witnesses, deputies, reporters, and courthouse hangers-on. Families on both sides of the aisle brought their lunch in paper sacks and ate in the courtroom. Every day it was standing room only in district court.

When there is no jury in a North Carolina District Court, the judge becomes the arbiter of the community's conflicts, much like a medieval magistrate, and a trial can take on the spontaneity of a town meeting. A judge asks a packed courtroom for information about a high school boy accused of fighting: "Can anyone here tell me about this boy?" A teacher in the back of the court gets up and, without approaching the bench, tells a horror story of the boy's home life, at which point the assistant DA, Adam, says, "Judge, I have no interest in prosecuting this young man." And that is that. Next case.

One of his DA friends remembers that whenever Adam was bored by the parade of cases in district court, he would slip upstairs and loiter outside superior court, as if hoping to be "discovered" and assigned to a more challenging case. It didn't happen until, Atticus-like, he claimed a case no one else on the DA's staff would touch—the rape of a prostitute who had a history of trading sex for drugs. Nobody wanted the case because it was unwinnable.

The victim, who by now had straightened out her life and was working at the local Burger King, was understandably afraid to testify. Adam met her every day at the Burger King and encouraged her to stand up for herself. Finally, she agreed, and in open court she gave the testimony Adam was hoping for: "Who would believe me?" she asked dramatically. "I was low, you know. But I could say this and say it good—no matter how low a person in the street, no one has the right to rape them."

He got a conviction for her and never worked downstairs again.

As a district attorney, he occupied a tiny office in the courthouse, where he did one-on-one interviews with murderers and pored over gruesome autopsy photos of their victims. He sat behind his desk and listened sympathetically to the pain and hatred of the victims' families. His paralegal remembers watching him cry with the parents of a child who had been killed by gunfire. He himself had never touched a gun and was spooked at the prospect of handling weapons in court. He secretly went to a firing range for the sole purpose of touching a few guns before having to enter one into evidence. When he did, one of the DAs remembers that he held it with two fingers like a dirty diaper.

His mother always called him "tenderhearted," a trait we attributed to his childhood struggle with illness. But by his thirtieth birthday, Tracy and I noticed that he was developing a callus against the sheer volume of small-town crime. Sometimes he acted like a tough guy and pretended not to care. The crust split open one day when he lost a case he should have won. A woman's boyfriend was accused of killing her child by punching him to death. A forensic expert testified that the child's extensive injuries, including broken ribs and a ruptured bowel, could not have been the result of a fall as the man claimed. The jury refused to convict, and the family of the accused, ignoring the judge's gavel pounding and the essential tragedy of the moment, celebrated in the courtroom afterward. Adam accused them of dancing on the little boy's grave and left the building red-eyed and angry.

Still, it was in Wilson that he found his place in the larger scheme of things. He delighted in being a small-town DA, even if his Atticus moments were few and far between. The notion that he was a public person whose actions mattered to the community and whose comments were quoted in the local newspaper gave him a great deal of satisfaction. He kept a scrapbook of his cases, as if his assorted rapes, murders, and assaults were memories of prom night.

He made a lot of friends among his colleagues, who in a small southern town were defined not by their respective law schools but by who their daddies were and where they had gone to high school. He liked to tell me about a judge who presided over a trial in which his son and his niece were the opposing attorneys. One day when we were eating barbeque at his "very favorite" restaurant, a greasy spoon with a smoking pig cooker out back, he proudly introduced me to the entire spectrum of the Wilson legal community, including the bartender whom he had sent away eighteen months earlier for breaking and entering.

After five years in Wilson, Adam and Jenny moved to Durham where Adam joined Tracy's law firm as an associate. At first I felt a little envious of the daily interactions of mother and son. They sent each other memos, and he began accompanying her to depositions and sitting second chair at her hearings. They did lunch. Sometimes he gave his opening and closing arguments on our patio while his mother took notes at the picnic table. They were having vocational conversations about the law the way he and I had once carried on about religion, baseball, and women, and I wasn't party to them.

I told Tracy I couldn't imagine a mother and son working together professionally (but I wouldn't have minded the arrangement myself). I asked her, "What's it like? I mean, how do you act in the office?"

"Oh, it's lovely," she giggled. "We act just like lawyers."

"What does he call you in front of clients?"

"What do you think he calls me? *Mom.*"

About a year ago, I stopped in at the Durham courthouse to look around and get the feel of it again. One of the court stenographers knew there was more to my visit than nostalgia. She told one of her coworkers that Adam's daddy was looking for him. That is the way southerners talk about unhappy fathers and their lost boys. All I wanted was a couple of minutes to stand in the back and watch. It was the end of the day, and a young lawyer in a wrinkled white shirt and narrow tie was holding forth in a near-empty courtroom. He was trying to explain to the defendant's mother why communicating threats is a serious offense, and to the judge why it doesn't deserve jail time. It could have been Adam.

The stenographer made a transcript of the Bo Dye trial and sent it to me along with the audiotape of Adam's closing argument. She must have known that listening to the tape would be difficult, for she enclosed this message on a pink Hallmark card: "I hope you find joy and peace in hearing

Adam's voice. Just imagine that he is expressing his love for all of you through this. Carolyn."

I read the transcript in one sitting. It introduced me to the stock characters that make for a good courtroom drama: the wise judge, the idealistic young lawyer, the rogue witness, the good prostitute. The court reporter is not allowed to sanitize the street language or correct mispronunciations. The transcript captures the stammered, broken sentences of lawyers and witnesses under pressure as well as the rush of unrehearsed eloquence. On the printed page, the ordinary repetition of *Yes sir / No sir / Yes / Yes / No / Never* conveys the rhythms of accidental poetry. The transcript is a frozen section of a terrible moment, when crimes are once again exposed and lives hang in the balance.

The audiotape reminds me of his acting days. On it his voice fills the courtroom as if it were a theater at UNC. I listen raptly to his closing argument in which he asks how the state could fail to produce credible witnesses from a street filled with spectators. "Well . . . my God," he cries theatrically, "where are they? Bo Dye is on trial for his life. Where are these people?" He allows just enough silence for the outrage of his question to sink in with the jury, whose good, earnest faces I can only imagine.

He concludes with a terrible allegory. Since the prosecution always goes last in closing, he begs the jury "to hold in your hearts all I have said to you," "for I will not have another opportunity to talk to you." Then he sits down.

On the tape you can hear the sound of his footsteps, the shuffle of papers, and the scrape of his chair on the floor. At which point the recording breaks off.

. . .

The jury deliberated seven hours. When it sent back a question to the judge about the state's burden to disprove self-defense, Adam thought it looked good for Bo Dye. The verdict of not guilty was read at 10:32 a.m. on March 31, 2005, and it hit the papers the next day.

Adam and Jenny capped his triumph with a week's vacation in Puerto Vallarta, a trip that had been delayed because of his interferon treatments sixteen months earlier. They went scuba diving, visited the mounds at Ixtapa, and on their last night asked a stranger to take their photograph. Upon their return, Adam had his regular three-month checkup at Duke Medical Center, and his life suddenly changed.

Not long after, a lawyer friend from Wilson called to congratulate him on his verdict in the Dye case. "It was in all the papers," he gushed. "Folks out here have you figured for a rising star." He was dumbfounded when Adam told him that he was sick and he was finished with the law. He said, "Now my life will take another path." This last report came to Tracy and me in an e-mail, but I can hear Adam delivering his line soberly with just the right combination of courage and regret, as Atticus might have done.

"Life changes fast." Joan Didion opens *The Year of Magical Thinking* with a sentence so unremarkable that it borders on the obvious. As she tells it, just before dinner her husband made a comment on the relative merits of single-malt versus double-malt Scotch—and suddenly he was dead on the floor.

Yes, life does change fast. But the real mystery is how quickly we adjust. How deftly we master the art of losing and come to terms with what, only yesterday, would have been unthinkable. If you need proof that we are nothing more than a handful of dust, notice how readily we adapt our soaring dreams to the ordinary stations of the earth.

One day you are at the top of your game, and lawyers in expensive suits are stopping you on busy corridors to shake your hand. The next day you are finished, and everyone at the courthouse knows it.

One day you are drinking Mexican coolers with a beautiful woman as you watch the sun set over Banderas Bay and the *camarero* is taking your picture. The next day you are waiting with your *dad,* of all people, in a bunker somewhere deep in Nuclear Medicine, where the woman who is carrying your unborn baby dare not sit hip to hip beside you with her arm locked desperately through yours, because the tracers they have sprayed into your bloodstream will pollute the entire waiting room, deform your child, and turn your present numbness into howling grief.

And yet when we stepped into this building and made our way through its color-coded zones and caught the blue elevator down to our destination in the sub-basement, we did not in fact balk or brace our bodies in the doorframe to resist the terror that was about to befall us. We didn't weep or make a big deal of it. We walked in as if we were running an errand to the bank or post office, determined to be pleasant even if the service was slow and the lines were long.

It wasn't that long ago that we were living on the surface of the earth with a view of the sky. We had never heard of temozolomide or oxycodone. We had not mastered the distinction between whole-brain and stereotactic radiation. We could not use the phrase "biologic immunotherapy" in a sentence. But now we had it all by rote, which is to say without grasping the science or complexity of any of it, the way a child who can't tell time says, "Just give me five more minutes."

Adam's rejections by NIH and other prominent cancer centers were already history. And so we settled in at Duke, the university we loved and trusted above all others. Adam was a child of its playing fields, gracious arches, and late afternoon shadows. Without the inconvenience of leaving, we had come home.

His PET scan completed, Adam and I walked out of Nuclear Medicine with our spirits intact. Nothing had changed and nothing frightening had happened, which had become my new definition of a good day. Following the arrows in the floor, we made our way through the labyrinth of treatment rooms and offices into the dingy hallways of the original hospital in the old Davison building.

With its interchangeable corridors and matching clinics, the hospital's layout represents only a small section of the labyrinth. There is the cancer itself, with the false hopes it engenders and its hard barrier-walls of suffering. Cancer also raises deeper religious and philosophical questions about the puzzle of existence and the moves required to solve it. Still, for all its complications, the labyrinth leads to an actual destination. If you pray your way through it, a labyrinth, or its guiding spirit, will take you to a quiet place at its center.

We emerged from Davison as from a New York subway into the bloom of a North Carolina spring day. Adam said he felt like walking, so we walked. We headed south on the Academic Quad, down the sandstone steps from Davison through a necropolis of blue, cream, and rust-colored stone buildings. Oak tassels were helicoptering in the air, piling up in stairwells and entrances to buildings. Leafing sycamore and willow oak spread above us; azalea, tulips, impatiens, and daffodils were in full bloom, perfectly sculpted as if for a funeral blanket. We walked past Old Chem and along the gallery of the Undergraduate Reading Room toward the crossroads of West Campus.

The time for exploring new terrain was over. We knew where to find the quiet part of the day.

At the crossroads we stood with a view of the chapel to our right and the Divinity School to its right. They are joined at the chapel's flank by an arcade through which mounds of pink, yellow, and white flowers made a bonfire against the church's north transept.

He wanted to see my new office, which is perched above the portico of the Divinity School, so we passed beneath a six-story magnolia and went up a flight of stairs. It was nothing but an empty room awaiting books, furniture, and the usual mementos that junk up an academic's office. It smelled of new carpet and paint. The painters had left the leaded windows open. "Oh, this is nice," he said. "It's so bright." We didn't chat about the law, the Dye case, or the many other things that had disappeared without a trace, as one might avoid mention of a disastrous first marriage or a stint in prison. Everything he said registered my accomplishments. Not one word acknowledged the probability of a future except, "You're going to like it here." At the thought of it he smiled at me, and I realized that I was no longer looking for something of *me* in him. Instead, a line from the story of Jacob and Esau popped into my head, where Jacob says to his brother, "Your face is like the face of God to me."

I shyly studied my own son's face. He was content with the goodness of the day, and therefore so was I. We had had our share of moments like this before, when the fish have quit biting or the game has wiped us out, when so little is happening that time seems to stand still. We were on one of our many expeditions, Adam and I, looking at ordinary things through one another's eyes. Taken together, these little outings added up to what he and I would have considered our life, which was nothing more complicated than being together uneventfully.

From the chapel tower the university carillonneur had begun his daily performance. The music was streaming through my windows like sunlight. The room glowed pale green from the trees and yellow from the pollen and orange in the late-afternoon sun. There in that unfurnished tomb of an office, bathed in its strange light and familiar melodies, all the usual attributes of the flesh gave way to incandescence. The radiance belonged to him, above all, but also to the two of us and to the room and the sacredness of the hour.

I wanted it never to end.

8

When he first learned the extent of his cancer, Adam made several moves in rapid succession. He began planning for his daughter's future. He quit his job. He got rid of his cell phone. He threw a clock off the back deck of his house into the creek below. Then he arranged to have himself admitted to the Eucharist in the Catholic Church.

His exploration of Catholicism had begun almost from the moment he met Jenny. In fact, I can't think of his new faith apart from his new love. He was living in Washington and completing his final weeks of law school at American University. She was an occupational therapist working with children with learning disabilities at the Lab School in Georgetown. He had moved from seminary housing to an apartment on Connecticut Avenue. She was living in a fourth-floor walk-up a few blocks away on Wisconsin across the street from the

National Cathedral. A mutual friend fixed them up on a blind date. It was April 17, 1998.

When she opened her door to meet him, Jenny would have come face-to-face with a tall, nervous stranger. He would have introduced himself with a one-liner to make her laugh and put them both at ease. Depending on the light in the hall, he might have been the leading man in a romantic comedy or maybe the leading man's funny best friend—but with nothing devious or even mischievous in his smile and with something approaching comfort in his enormous, deep-set eyes. Old-fashioned hair the color of winter wheat, long, swept and tumbling, parted haphazardly near the middle.

He had the broad nose of both his grandfathers and the Lincolnesque cheekbones of no one in the family. When he smiled, the corners of his mouth reached for the lobes of his ears. No doubt he shaved that night, but if he hadn't, no one would have noticed. He was wearing a gray silk shirt, fine-gauge tan pants that sat casually on his hips, with a skinny belt from the '50s. Not quite The Territory Ahead, but it worked for him.

That night they drank margaritas at the Cactus Cantina a few blocks up Wisconsin Avenue and shot pool afterward. The next day Adam called a couple of women he had been dating to tell them he had found someone permanent. On their second date they went to Mass at Jenny's parish, Holy Trinity in Georgetown. They saw one another the next forty-one consecutive days, and that was it. By the time Tracy and I met her at his graduation, we knew she was the one. He had left instructions that Jenny was to be seated with his sister Sarah and on no condition between his mother and father. He was leaving nothing to chance.

A year later, almost to the day, he went to the Durham courthouse and had his name changed: he added Jenny's maiden name, Ewers, to the names we had given him at his baptism. He said, "If she insists on taking my name, I'll take hers, too." Three days later they got married. I gave the homily at their wedding in a Catholic church in downtown Charlotte; a priest performed the ceremony.

Before the service began, Adam and I paced the corridor behind the church's reredos, he in his black tux, me in my white alb and red stole for Pentecost. I was trying to settle him down, and he was trying to settle me down. We were using ridiculous sports analogies, as if one of us was a seasoned catcher and the other a high-strung pitcher.

"It helps to breathe. Take a deep breath. You'll find it relaxes you."

"*You* take a deep breath."

"I *am* breathing."

"Let's both just take it easy and do it."

Then he opened the door onto the chancel to meet his bride. It was a moment in time, yet one that will always remain cleanly and eternally out of time. I followed him through the door and we formed our wedding tableau before the altar. Jenny wore a satin A-line dress with a beaded halter and a train of scalloped lace. Her smile was veiled and mysterious. He gazed at her as if dumbfounded by his good luck.

My sermon was about the grace of marriage. It was okay except for a comment I made near the end: "Someday, Adam and Jenny, someday you will be old. Still cute, but old. And at your sixtieth wedding anniversary you will hold hands and ask, 'How did we get so lucky?' But what you will really mean is, 'How gracious God has been to us.'"

I think preachers should speak only what they have been given to say and not one word more. They should not pretend to have a privileged view of the future. They should hold something back against the night.

The sermon ended with the same sign and blessing given at Adam's baptism: "Jennifer and Adam, may the Lord preserve your going out and your coming in from this time forth and forevermore."

And suddenly they were slow dancing, her head on his shoulder, at the center of an admiring ballroom, in the very eye of their magical life.

A few days later we received a postcard from them during their honeymoon in which they thanked me for the homily. Adam added a postscript: "Jenny and I have been married 48 hours. So far, no problems."

Adam began receiving instruction in Catholicism when he and Jenny lived in Wilson, but he was put off by the priest's anti-Protestant notions and gave it up. By the time they moved to Durham in the spring of 2004, five years after their wedding, everything had changed. He had been operated on and undergone treatments for cancer, and now that the interferon was out of his system, he and Jenny were trying to get pregnant.

In Durham, they found the perfect parish, the enormous Immaculate Conception Church, a congregation served by

Franciscan friars located in the gritty space between the always-under-construction Immaculata School and the Emily Krzyzewski Family Life Center. Half a block from the church, a line of storefronts housed the Pentecostal Tabernacle of Joy, a cab company, a head shop, and Ar-Razzaq Islamic Center. The makeup of the congregation mirrored the economic and racial contests going on in its neighborhood, a sophisticated microcosm of America, where Anglos, African Americans, and Latinos struggled to make a decent life. Every Sunday the people at Immaculate Conception asked God to bring the soldiers home from Iraq and to protect the immigrants who work in the hog factories and chicken processing plants of North Carolina. Every Sunday its intercessions included a prayer for "those who bear the suffering of Christ," which is a black or Latina mother trying to support her children on a domestic's wages, an unemployed or undocumented manual laborer, or a person with cancer who is too sick to work. The church's ministry of justice was a perfect match for Adam's own convictions, especially its work with prisoners and its opposition to the death penalty. Once he got to know the priests, he began coordinating his work on behalf of his jailed clients with the church's ministry to them. He also hired a tutor and began learning Spanish.

The two priests Adam and Jenny knew best were Rev. David McBriar, a seventy-year-old social firebrand with a white buzz-cut and a PhD in theology from Toronto, and Rev. Steve Patti, a younger contemplative thinker whose homilies were laced with allusions to literature and film, and who would eventually become Adam's confessor. David immediately took to Adam, pressing him in several discussions to explain his opposition to the death penalty. Adam spoke with him about what he called "the inequities of the law and the absolutes of the gospel." When Jesus abolished the law of retribution for his followers, he abolished it for his followers who happen to be legislators, lawyers, and judges, too. Father David, who regularly led demonstrations on behalf of immigrants and underpaid workers, saw a younger, kindred spirit in his newest parishioner. David was also taken by what he would later call Adam's "wry humor." "This is what I asked him," David reported to me, his Irish eyes smiling: "'Are *all* your clients on death row?' He says to me, 'Not yet, Father, not yet.'"

Adam's decision to become a Catholic was never the subject of a vocational conversation, at least not with me, except on matters of the Eucharist and baptism. He wanted to know how Protestants, Lutherans, and Catholics differ on the Lord's Supper. I told him that for many Protestants the communion elements symbolize the presence of Jesus in the sacrament but that Lutherans and Catholics believe that he's really there, so much so that for Catholics the presence of Jesus obliterates or transforms the reality of the bread and wine. We were walking Sadie in Rockwood Park across the road from his house in Durham. I was giving a strolling lecture punctuated by many seminary words. Adam took it all in and, throwing a stick for Sadie, made short work of it: "So, for Protestants—not enough Jesus in the bread and wine; Catholics have too much Jesus in the bread and wine; and Lutherans—just right. When it comes to Jesus, can it ever be wrong to have 'too much'?"

We shifted gears. "Now Adam, about baptism," I said, "don't forget, you are already baptized. You are already a member of Christ's church." No doubt, I was thinking of the pre–Vatican II practice of re-baptizing converts from Protestantism. I spoke to him about re-baptism the way parents warn their teenagers about sex and drugs.

"Dad, this isn't the Dark Ages. There will be no re-baptism." Then he added, as if repeating his catechism, "I am a baptized child of God."

Adam's interest in Catholicism originated in his notions of marriage. He not only reveled in being married; he reveled in the *idea* of being married. He would bellow, "Honey, I'm home," as he walked in the door at night, parodying the conventional life he wouldn't have minded living for another fifty years. On the things that matter, a husband and wife belong together, and he knew the Eucharist mattered. When he got involved with Immaculate Conception and its mission, his family-driven interest in Catholicism quickly grew into genuine devotion to a particular congregation and its priests. Then he met Bo Dye, and his frequent visits to the Durham County Jail took on a distinctly pastoral flavor as he discovered a new way to be a good Catholic.

Adam was well into his instruction at Immaculate Conception when he received his final diagnosis. His confirmation was scheduled for Pentecost, about a month away. On April 15 my friend and colleague Teresa Berger called Adam to tell him she had heard the news and wanted to help. She was a member of the parish and had only met Adam a few times, but she immediately embraced him as her personal responsibility. "What do you want me to do for you?" she asked.

Without hesitation he replied, "I want to receive the Eucharist with my wife."

The following Monday morning Adam was received into the Catholic Church by the rite of confirmation. "A perfect day for a Lutheran to become a Catholic," Teresa said to me under her breath, "since there is no pope." (John Paul had died two weeks before.)

The brief ceremony took place in the Daily Mass Chapel to the side of the main sanctuary before a congregation of about fifty people. The service unfolded in a few simple movements beneath an enormous replica of the San Damiano Cross in Assisi. It was a cross Tracy and I knew well, since a small replica purchased on our honeymoon had hung in a succession of our apartments and houses over the years. Tracy, Sarah, and I participated in the rite and laid hands on Adam's head as we prayed him into the Catholic Church and into the hope of a greater life to come. Jenny was his sponsor, and Tracy's brother, Regan, who had flown down from New Jersey, read one of the lessons. In his homily Father David spoke extemporaneously but eloquently of the dialectic of God's absence and God's presence. In his prayer he gave thanks to God for Adam's baptism in the Lutheran Church.

That took me back to the cold Sunday morning in the country, when he wore my father's lace dress and I marked him with the universal sign of suffering. When it's a baby being baptized, the ceremony's language of death has a faraway, metaphoric ring. But now the terrible promise of baptism had come into focus, and we could make out the substance of the metaphor. What a long journey it had been from the little church on the prairie to a place named Immaculate Conception with its holy water, Stations of the Cross, and electric-blue shrine to Our Lady of Guadalupe. Once again we were setting our son adrift on a dangerous sea, now as a man and no longer a baby, but still our child and a child of God.

Adam, for his part, seemed profoundly thankful to receive the Eucharist with his wife. *Adam,* Father David said with great resonance, *Body of Christ,* and placed the Host on his tongue.

Smiling and somewhat subdued after Mass, Adam was perfectly at ease as he moved about the narthex greeting worshipers. Despite the casual atmosphere of daily Mass, he had dressed for the occasion in his lawyer-gray suit, white shirt, and apricot tie, the same suit he had worn at his swearing in as an assistant district attorney four years earlier. He was still sporting the designer-stubble he had grown in Puerto Vallarta.

We have a framed photograph from his swearing-in ceremony in the courtroom. He is looking directly into the camera and smiling confidently, as if he knows something the camera doesn't. It is a picture of what C. P. Snow called the "time of hope," when a young man's whole life stretches before him and anything is possible. On the basis of that photo, one can have no doubt that he will master his new vocation, win his cases, and make a name for himself.

In the photo taken on the chancel steps after his confirmation, he is still smiling, but his smile betrays more than a trace of vulnerability. He looks like a man who no longer holds the future in his hands but has placed himself into the receivership of friends. He has just laid his body on the altar of something larger than himself. Clearly, there are things he does not know. He is awaiting revelation. Those to either side of him in the photo are smiling extra-radiantly, as if to compensate for the lack of sparkle in his eyes and to mask the essential sadness of the day.

That morning I walked the Stations of the Cross in the main sanctuary of Immaculate Conception, stood at the bubbling baptismal font near the entrance, checked out the Shrine of Our Lady of Guadalupe, and peered in at the Host housed in its tabernacle in the mysterious alcove behind the altar. The place felt like a gymnasium to me, loaded with physical equipment and things to do—a place where Adam would go into training again and run the race that lay before him.

Thomas Merton once said, "Souls are like athletes that need opponents worthy of them, if they are to be tried and extended and pushed to the full use of their powers." Merton's comment has been co-opted by the self-help industry in America, but he was not talking about the frontiers of human potential but the grace of godly dying. He was speaking of his father's heroic struggle with a brain tumor and the suffering he endured, about which he added, "It was making him great."

Now Adam, too, had discovered an opponent that would push him to the full use of his powers. A road had been revealed to him. Actually, two distinct paths opened before him: one would take him through the maze of chemo and radiation to an uncertain end. The other, originating in his baptism and nurtured by the rituals of his newfound community, would lead him through the labyrinth to his true destination.

It would make him "great."

9

Modern cancer treatment is itself a ritual from which the sacred dimension has been removed. It prescribes a rigid schedule of activities that is oddly *like* a religion and one that operates according to a quasi-sacred logic, but from which something crucial is missing. Cancer treatment puts you on its own cycle of depletion and rebirth: every week it kills you a little in order to give you life; every week it brings you to the edge of despair in order to prepare you for the possibility of good news. And before you know it, you are a devout member of a church you never meant to join. You become an expert in recognizing the vestments of its high priests and the stigmata of its saints. You learn how to move your body through the color-coded stations—from dermatology to radiology to oncology to hematology to the treatment suite and out the glass doors to the parking deck.

Soon you enter a new linguistic world and acquire a specialized vocabulary. Not only do you master the names of unfamiliar drugs and treatments, but you learn new and more careful ways of using the old words. You develop a rich thesaurus of synonyms and circumlocutions for death. You say, "If I'm out of the picture," or "If I'm not around," instead of "When I die." You translate your childhood belief in divine miracles into an equally fervent belief in medical miracles. You retain your ability to hope, but you learn to prune that hope with tasteful realism.

You become habituated to your new church's practices with such devotion that even the slightest deviation deranges your universe and produces spasms of anxiety. "The saline solution is *always* administered *after* the Taxol and carboplatin. Why did she give the two together? My treatment always takes three hours. Today it took only two hours and forty minutes. What can this possibly mean?"

The religion of cancer treatment holds out the carrot of survival. It confuses the prolongation of life with salvation. If you live exactly sixty months plus a day, you will be numbered among the saved.

Many cancer specialists speak of the disease in language once reserved for the devil or mortal sin. In the best-selling *How We Die,* Yale surgeon Sherwin Nuland raises the curtain on a scene of such depravity that Calvinism appears optimistic by comparison. In his chapter "The Malevolence of Cancer," he denounces "our old enemy," which, "far from being a clandestine foe, is in fact berserk with the malicious exuberance of killing." "Its first cells," he continues, "are the bastard offspring of unsuspecting parents who ultimately reject them because they are ugly, deformed, and unruly."

Faced with this stinking bastard of a foe, the victim's response must be equally aggressive. But there is a catch. The object of our hatred is a part of the patient's own body. Cancer does not invade from the outside; it is a palace rebellion among the body's own Praetorian Guard. The fighter's instinct is a powerful motivational tool, but by giving the disease a *persona* and pretending it has conscious drives and malevolent purposes, we demonize our very selves.

And when the battle is won, as it is with an increasing number of cancers, what then? The successful treatment of those whose only metaphor has been *fight* or, in the language of one online survivor, *kick butt,* leaves the victors with no vocabulary with which to thank God or express astonishment at the grace of being alive.

One of the unintended consequences of the jihad on cancer is that the cancer specialist, with years invested in sophisticated weapons research, attacks the disease but fails to treat the person. The disease has the single surname, cancer, while those who suffer from it are legion with a multitude of needs and stories. The individual's identity subtly shifts from that of a person to a site for observation, treatment, and further study of the disease. And when the barbarian horde of invaders finally takes over, as it did in Adam's case, and the battle begins to go badly, the first person to retreat is often the oncologist, who abandons his or her patient to the palliative-care people and disappears from the patient's life.

Adam began his treatment with a dermatologist in Wilson who quickly referred him to a surgeon in Durham from whom he was sent to an oncologist, and thence to a second dermatologist, a radiologist, a hematologist, another oncologist, and several other specialists in diet and pain relief. Each addressed the appropriate sector of Adam's body with utmost professionalism. Devotion to their work was never an issue. What was missing from this parade of specialists was an abiding center, a *physician,* whose very title bears age-old cultural and even religious resonances, whose care for my son would persist through his many treatments and the rapidly descendant stages of his life. I yearned for someone with the vision to see him whole, and the compassion to see him through.

A young oncology fellow named Tim came closest to fulfilling this role during Adam's illness. He and Adam became friends, and Tim was willing to allow his human feelings for Adam to penetrate the veil that often separates doctor and patient. He was in the room when the oncologist outlined the treatment options for metastatic melanoma. Only a few hours earlier, before the final round of tests had begun, it was Tim who made the rare (for a physician) declaration: "You are cured, Adam. I just *know* it." From a scientific standpoint, he could not have been more wrong; from a human one, he spoke the heart's truth. A few weeks later, his rotation ended, and as Adam entered a new phase of treatment Tim moved on to a new specialization in another city.

Against the "malicious exuberance" of the enemy, medical science pursues its own version of the nuclear option. Whole-brain radiation is administered when the cancerous lesions and cells have diffused throughout the brain. Radiation is no respecter of cells; it incinerates the good with the bad, the healthy along with the malignant. In the brain perfectly good cells are thrown into the fire along with their destructive brothers and sisters.

The side effects of whole-brain radiation rival the symptoms of the disease itself: skin irritation, hair loss, hearing problems, nausea, loss of appetite, growth defects, neurological impairment—and more brain cancer. Longer-term effects include confusion, problems with memory, and personality changes. Half of those who survive for two years are affected by dementia.

If whole-brain radiation is successful in curtailing the growth of the cancer or reducing it to a few defined tumors, stereotactic radiation may send its laser-guided knife into the crosshairs of the tumor itself. A National Cancer Institute study determined that brain radiation alone produces a median overall survival rate of 12.1 months. When radiation is combined with a powerful and expensive drug marketed as Temodar, the median overall survival rate for those with metastases to the brain soars to 14.6 months, a gain of 2.5 months. For those whose melanoma has spread to the liver, bone, and brain, as it had in Adam's body, the median life expectancy is 4.4 months.

The immediate effect of Adam's two forms of treatment followed the medical literature point for point. The skin on his face and head was left reddened and burned. He suffered the predicable nausea, exhaustion, and hair loss. He began moving and speaking at a slower pace, but his mental ability was not impaired. By the end of his treatment cycle, he was too weak to drive or walk the dogs.

The dialectic of dying in order to live originated on ancient slaughter stones. Its logic continues as the essence of traditional cancer treatment. It is hard to imagine that future generations will not associate the devastating effects of chemotherapy and radiation with the age of "Heroic Medicine" in the seventeenth and eighteenth centuries. One day these treatments will join bloodletting, intestinal purging, blistering, and prefrontal lobotomies in the museum of dangerous and discredited therapies.

In the meantime, such treatments are keeping people alive who would have otherwise died. I hear the grateful testimony to chemotherapy and radiation from dozens of acquaintances, whose lymphomas, brain tumors, and breast cancers have been successfully treated and whose diseases have migrated from the hopelessly "terminal" side of the ledger to the "treatable" and even the "chronic." I see them with their hair grown back and spirits restored, their lives extended beyond their wildest dreams. I watch them go hiking on the Appalachian Trail and take their children to Disney World. My closest friend writes of his grandchild's treatment for brain cancer: "Sighs of relief and thankfulness to God for a miracle called radiation."

The treatment suite in the Morris Cancer Clinic was a series of low-ceilinged rooms with no windows and no medical equipment to speak of except for two nurses' stations and a forest of IV poles. The individual rooms were crowded with beige Barcaloungers grouped at odd angles and arranged like displays in a furniture store. Each patient was permitted one companion who was seated in a straight chair beside the recliner.

Scores of patients were jammed into tight quarters; yet the suite's most memorable characteristic was its eerie silence.

Conversation was nonexistent or deeply muffled, as if the walls were constructed of leather and the floors of cork. The room reminded me of a lock ward designed to help its inmates absorb the unabsorbable. A few curtained alcoves held beds for those too weak to sit for their treatment.

Some of the patients showed up in sweats, as if to treat these few hours as grunge time or a trip to the gym. Others dressed for the occasion in order to meet the enemy at their very best. Some read or chatted quietly with a friend or spouse, while others, like Adam, dissociated from the scene around them and slept. Adam slept aggressively as if willing the room into nonexistence.

One day a middle-aged woman dressed in a clown suit with an orange wig, rouge, and bulbous nose walked through the suite. She stopped at each recliner to offer cookies and juice and to make small talk. I felt for her; she was probably a well-intentioned volunteer, but the clown thing just wasn't working. As she passed Adam's chair, he opened his eyes long enough to see the source of the moving shadow, then closed them again and turned away from the lady clown and into himself with a hardened absence of expression I had never seen in him.

For all his powers of dissociation, Adam managed to befriend a fellow patient, a man in his midthirties who was being treated for advanced cancer. He was falling apart with fear and worry for his wife and child. When Adam met him he seemed to be having an anxiety attack, repeating again and again, "I can't do this, man, I can't do this." He said he was considering ending his treatment and committing suicide. I heard Adam say, "Give it three days and you'll feel better. I promise you." After that, he always looked for the fellow in the treatment suite and continued to encourage him.

During his weeks at Duke I kept my eye peeled for fathers like me with children in treatment. I spied a man my age with a son who might have been a few years younger than Adam. The younger man was wan and white and completely bald. He wore a white V-neck t-shirt every day and bleached-out trousers. He moved around the suite as if he were made of porcelain. I paid close attention to the father's eyes, how they followed his son with militant sadness. Whenever the boy moved, the father moved with him just to his left and a little behind him. They were like two dancers who have been together a long time. I tried to picture Adam and me at that stage, when I would be the custodian of his pale shadow and we too would move as one. But when I succeeded in imagining it, I frantically blocked the thought of it.

I only saw these people—the scared young man, the pale boy and his father, the clown, the nurses—within the closed universe of the treatment center. Never in the parking deck, the supermarket, or a restaurant. Never above ground in the land of the living. Once I did run into one of Adam's doctors on a Saturday morning in a local diner. He was sitting at the counter eating breakfast with his little boy. We were so amazed to see each other out of context we hardly knew what to say. How could he be the unquestioned authority on all things, and I the supplicant father of a dying child, when we were sitting across the counter from each other eating oatmeal?

The treatment of cancer is one of the last bastions of segregation. It takes place in a secret Zombie Church with low, leaded rooms, coffin-like scanners, draughts of poison, and skeletal dancers. First, you enter it; then it enters you and possesses you. "I am in the hospital even when I am outside the hospital," a cancer patient complained, reflecting on the mental tyranny of cancer. Flannery O'Connor once wrote that being sick was like visiting another country. Inevitably, however, the place to visit becomes your place to live. One day Tracy and I were sitting in the hematology lab waiting for Adam when she said without elaborating, "We are really *in* it, aren't we?"

The very word "cancer" infects our language and imagination. If you want to say the worst about any crime, blight, or prejudice, you will call it a "cancer" on the body politic. And the one with cancer—genuine cellular cancer in his actual physical body—bears not only the disease but the weight of all its ugly associations. Susan Sontag, a onetime cancer survivor herself, was right: there really is nothing more punitive than to give a disease a meaning. The one with cancer *becomes* a cancer on the human community, a byword, whose plight is whispered by all who pass by:

> *Terminal,*
> *thin*
> *sick*
> *so young,*
> *so sad*
> *so sorry,*
> *(did he smoke?)*
> *Shh.*

Most cancer patients respond to their disease in one of two ways. Some heroically continue their daily routines as best they can, rearranging their work according to the rhythms of chemotherapy and the necessary downtime for recovery. You see them in their bandanas, baseball caps, wigs, and shawls, carefully selecting the ripest avocado in the store or quietly catching their breath between tasks at the office. They squeeze the simplest pleasures from each livable day. They cut the lawn or play nine holes and take a nap; they defy the devil and go dancing, then take it slow the rest of the week.

Others go into semi-seclusion, perhaps because they have sensed the recoil among healthy people to those who are thin, pale, and hairless. As Kafka said of the reactions to his own terminal illness (tuberculosis), "Everyone drops into a shy, evasive, glassy-eyed manner of speech." Those who are ill follow their schedule of treatments, but they are rarely seen outside the home and their circle of family and close friends. They endure by nesting with the disease.

There is an alternative to the shame and social isolation that many cancer sufferers experience. The best dying is done in community, if you can find the right community. Long ago when I was a pastor, a young woman came into my study one Sunday and asked somewhat aggressively, "What does this church have to offer me?" I should have paid closer attention to her eyes, but like a fool I reeled off the most attractive features of our program and facilities. She said, "Well, that's nice, but I'm looking for someone to help me die. Do you think your church is up to that? And what about you?" she asked, calling me out. "Is that something you could do?"

This is something the church is supposed to be good at. Its

liturgy welcomes everyone to the feast. "Come unto me, all you who labor and are heavy laden, and I will give you rest," Jesus says. "Eat and drink with us," we say. "You are no freak and we are not freaked out by your suffering." The liturgy of life offers the kiss of peace to everyone, including the pale, the scabrous, and the very skinny. We name and lament our diseases before God and do not conceal our bodies. We are not ashamed.

Cancer Church knows only two categories—dead and alive. Adam was looking for another category and another path. This is the path that ventures beyond survival (which is nothing to be sneezed at) and promises blessedness. When Jesus said, "Blessed are the pure in heart, for they shall see God," he was speaking of those who have followed the way of suffering and, despite the destructiveness of selected cells in their own bodies, have achieved a better ending than most would have thought possible. If they did clinical trials on blessedness, the researchers at NIH would discover that for some patients *health* is a two-way street. For just as good health is making its sloppy exit in bursting tumors and failing organs, another claimant to the title is arriving in the form of kindness, courage, and an inexplicable wholeness of the human spirit—what the Bible calls "health." They would discover two entangled histories: a scientifically charted history of the disease; and an enchanted, uncharted history of the person who bears it with grace.

Sanctuary

10

When Adam got rid of his clock and cell phone, it meant he was through with billable hours and consultations measured to the minute. By the time the pain got to the bone, it was impossible for him to work. There may be jobs one can do while loaded with OxyContin, but leaping up from a table and shouting, "Objection, your honor, move to strike!" is not one of them. In early May he arranged for others to take his cases, including his precious assignments from the Capital Defender Office, and walked out on his future with the lights still blazing.

By this time, Tracy had pegged her career to his and her love of the law to his passion for it. But now, there would be no more opening and closing arguments given on our patio, no more legal gossip, shared depositions, or mother-son mentoring sessions. The early mornings at Starbucks and the late-night brainstorming sessions with colleagues ended abruptly.

He and his mother, who had spent so many hours arguing the law and plotting his career, simply stopped acting like lawyers. Adam did not quit working, but he did change jobs. With his legal career over, he turned to another, more challenging line of work.

As a little boy he had been fascinated by palindromes, words or sentences that read the same forward or backward, and had wasted many hours trying to create new ones. He never tired of introducing himself to us as if he were the First Man presenting himself to Eve: "Madam I'm Adam." Then he grew up to become a palindrome himself, a young man whose life would make as much sense from its end as its beginning. Like Atticus, he already understood the importance of integrity in one's private and public life. Now he took the same wisdom and applied it to the end of life—his life. The conclusion should not be incidental to the plot, but essential to it—like the stories of the saints that *begin* with a rollicking good death and work backward, about which one asks, "What was it about his life that made his immolation necessary?" If one were to reverse-engineer the grace of Adam's last days, it would be necessary to work backward through the days of his suffering to the occasions on which he learned compassion and love, until at last one arrived at the day of his baptism, the day he was marked for death.

Soon after his diagnosis he began buying crosses, lots of them: Greek, Native American, St. Andrew's, Celtic, Coptic crosses, many of them handcrafted and threaded by a strand of rawhide. He had been brought up to value the cross, but now he embraced it as the symbol of his bond to Jesus: it was cancer and the cross, death and the cross, a lost family and the cross.

He had accepted a new and more definitive diagnosis: he was carrying a small corner of Christ's cross. He draped it around his neck and unselfconsciously kissed it with Latin adoration.

He showed me a small crucifix with a tiny silver Jesus mounted on a polished white disc; his little arms were open and extended but clearly overmatched by an immense world of suffering. "This one is so beautiful," he said, the way a beachcomber might describe the perfect abalone or scallop. He treated the crucifix as a *find,* as the very element that would alchemize his many losses into victory. Now he had become a part of that groaning immensity to which the little Jesus opened his arms.

Jenny seemed surprised by the intensity he brought to their religious devotions. "He had an instinct for what was real," she later told me. Adam's confessor wrote, "In those last few months he saw things with a deep clarity." Instead of retreating into childish patterns, as sometimes happens with the terminally ill, Adam took the lead and set the ground rules for the final season of his life. Dying well had become the young man's ultimate proof of competence. He confided to his uncle Regan, "You know, I am the only person in our family capable of doing this."

This.

He announced to Jenny, "We are going to use our time in a new way." The two of them went off the clock in earnest and began to live in another idiom. They began performing the small, repetitive actions by which clocktime is abolished and the eternal takes its place. Jenny was already at home in the world of Catholic devotion; Adam embraced it as if he had been looking for this sort of work his whole life. Now their days would be measured only by devotion to each other, kindness toward others, the rhythms of prayer, and the growth of her belly. Together they lit candles, said their prayers, recited the psalms, went to daily Mass, did the Stations, knelt at icons, watched old movies, ate pizza, and observed the stars from their deck, all according to a new standard of time that wasn't really time at all, but a heightened awareness of the interlocking spaces through which he had to move in order to reach his goal.

It doesn't do them justice to say that they were simply trying to bring some order into their lives, the way children and bored adults are often said to "need a routine." What they were doing was more original and countercultural. One thinks of the monastery, whose inhabitants do not live by the watch but by the sun and the moon and the bell. When the bell sounds, they rise to sing the psalms. When the sun begins to set, they stop working and prepare to pray and sleep. The monk doesn't sit in his cell and ask, "Where will I be sixty months from now?" As the prisoner Dietrich Bonhoeffer wrote, "I think that even in this place we ought to live as if we had no wishes and no future, and just be our true selves."

"Here is the way it is when I wake up," Adam said to me. We were sitting in the shade on his lower deck eating popsicles. This was a rare revelation of a scene from his marriage, the details of which he usually kept to himself. "Jenny's got these scented candles lit in our bedroom. She's standing there in her shorts, pregnant, fat and adorable, with a cup of Flor Essence for me. She pours the tea and then anoints me with water that her uncle brought back from Lourdes. I take my medication. Then we pray." He said it as if he were describing the morning workout.

As a college student, Adam read Simone Weil's *Waiting for God,* in which she writes to her confessor, "Only obedience is invulnerable for all time." Whether he remembered that sentence I don't know, but he and Jenny began to live as if it were the motto for the rest of his life. Unlike the philosophical arguments *about* God, obedience *to* God never occupies ambiguous or questionable territory in the spiritual life. When you practice obedience, it's like drafting behind someone else's energy. Christians have always been better at absorbing suffering than justifying it, anyway. They are better at walking the Stations of the Cross than explaining why there has to *be* a cross in each of our lives. They are better at praying than defending the efficacy of prayer. Instead of debating the usefulness of prayer, as Adam and I might have done in the old days, he and Jenny would simply pray for themselves and others.

The key to their praying was what Simone Weil called *attention.* Adam could see that his illness was creating ripples of suffering among his family and friends. Jenny tells me they kept a list of people who needed their prayers, with special attention given to those who were already grieving for him. Tracy's mother, Nina, who was being cared for in a nearby convalescent center, would have been on the list, as was Jenny's mom, Alice, who had recently been treated for breast cancer, and so were Tracy and his sister Sarah, and so was I.

I know from Jenny that the actual first thing Adam did in

the morning was talk to his unborn daughter. By sometime in early May he was able to address her by name, though her name would remain a closely guarded secret until the day she was born. He would ask the baby how she had slept, tell her funny stories, kiss her feet or fists (or whatever was protruding), but most of all he would remind her how much he loved her. They were alive at the same time on the same earth, he and his baby, and I imagine she knew his voice when she heard it calling to her each morning. At some unfathomed depth, she remembers it still.

They went to 8:15 Mass every morning at Immaculate Conception, about which Adam said to me, "It's the best part of the day."

On Wednesdays they attended Children's Mass with the kids of Immaculata School. The children came to know him as "Mr. Adam" and wrote him poems and drew him pictures in which he appears to tower over the other figures. One day several Latina second graders stood up and sang "Pues Si Vivimos" for him during the service. "How did that make you feel?" I asked. "It felt good," he said with uncharacteristic reserve.

He got to know the daily Mass crowd, and they cared about him deeply. He was endlessly patient when an elderly man from Italy presented him with a saint's relics from the old country. The presentation came with a long and pious history to which Adam nodded respectfully, "Yes sir. Yes sir."

Before Mass he would light candles at the base of a wooden icon depicting the Virgin and Child, and kneel there on the pavement and pray. One day Tracy met him for Mass at Immaculate Conception. As she approached the entrance she could see him through the window kneeling at the shrine. It was summer, and he was wearing a hooded Carolina warm-up. He was cold and on his knees, she says, framed in the church window. It was not good for her to see him that way. Now, she says to me with enormous restraint, "It's a memory."

I saw him pray that way too. He was kneeling at the base of a wooden plaque, a study in self-abandonment. The icon was embanked with flowers and candles and a few handwritten messages. In that moment he was utterly alone, and so was I. I never felt so far from him as on that morning when I stood within arm's reach of him, trying to pray with him but also torn apart by what I saw: my son on the hard bricks of Immaculate Conception, motionless, serene as a sanded statue, and lost in a realm I could not enter.

Late one morning, when Adam and I were sitting in the lower level of his house with nothing to do, he started talking about the Eucharist again. It was another of his monologues that began from a standing start, with no introduction. "If you have cancer and you want to give God a taste of the hell you are going through, you get down on your knees in front of a cross and tell him about it. Then you come to the altar and give God everything you have, and God gives you everything *He* has. That's how Father Steve puts it." We were no longer discussing the composition of the communion elements like a couple of scholastics; he was gathering steam like a street preacher, and he was good at it: "You say, 'This is my body,' and you bring it to the altar like a piece of bad meat, and God says, 'No, this is *my* body.' You come naked, and God dresses you. You come hungry, and God feeds you." His voice was full of rage and dare. He was preaching to himself, a hungering congregation of one, and to me as an afterthought. He was throwing himself into the face of God.

You bring your dirt to the table (he said "shit"), and God accepts it as something beautiful—the flesh of his Son. It wasn't a pious communion Adam was preaching about, but a primitive trade, as if at a scrap exchange, where you leave something old or broken and walk away with something better. You return again and again to that place until, finally, there's nothing left of the original *you,* and all that remains is the new thing that has been forming in you. Protestants call this transaction Communion or the Lord's Supper, Catholics and Lutherans call it Eucharist. A dying boy calls it "the best part of the day."

The philosopher Wittgenstein once said, "The human body is the best picture of the human soul." Most cancer patients would dispute that, but I do not, because cancer comes with a body and demands a bodily response. The dignity of some performances really does open a window onto the soul.

Occasionally, a member of Immaculate Conception says to me, "I can still see him sitting there in that pew with his head in his hands," and with their gestures they outline his form as if to sketch him back into the picture. It is then I realize that his body, the part of the human animal so many Christians think is unimportant, has carved out a special place in the memory of those who were with him.

The only time I disagree with Wittgenstein is when I read the radiology reports. Then I find myself despising the multiple lesions and nodules on his body and instead focusing on his spirit. Then I want to say, "No way was that body my son Adam." But it was.

In the *Paradiso,* Dante says that our bodies will be restored not only for our sakes alone but for the sake of those who loved our bodies.

A woman from the church said to me, "I can see him there—"

I impulsively interrupted her, "I wish you had known him the way I did, when he wasn't a victim." All I meant to say was that she should have known him in his "time of hope," which was how I wanted to remember him.

She pounced on my carelessness. "*No one* saw him as a victim. He was a *witness*." It was a genuine rebuke directed to me, his own flesh and blood, who of all people should have understood the power of his body and its meaning for others.

After daily Mass Adam and Jenny would go into the main sanctuary, an enormous, inviting space with a free-standing altar faced on three sides by square-backed open pews and kneelers, and they would pray there for about twenty minutes. On their way out they might dip their fingers in the holy water from the massive but simple stone baptismal font at the entrance to the sanctuary.

"Then we go to the Mad Hatter or Foster's for breakfast," he said. If he wasn't too tired, he and Jenny would shop for baby things on Ninth Street, Durham's version of a funky urban neighborhood. On other days—most days, at first— they went straight from church to radiation, until radiation was finally halted.

. . .

During those weeks I met him late each morning in the lower level of his house, in the recreation room where he kept his desk and books and a big TV. At the back of his recliner was a wall of books carefully tiered according to their intellectual heft and relevance to his life. If you studied their arrangement carefully, you could trace his steps from the time of hope to the new theory of timelessness he was working out in this half-buried room. On the top shelf were his law texts, including several books on the theory of justice; on the next his philosophy books; and below that his pleasure reading, made up of true crime books and whodunits. The bottom shelf represented the earnest, striving side of Adam: books on auto repair, martial arts, winning chess, winning basketball, a guide to writing fiction, harmonica playing, conversational Spanish, *Waiting for God,* how to be a decent Catholic, three books on parenting, and *Why Courage Matters* by John McCain.

I would usually find him settled into his recliner watching the NBA play-off game he had recorded the night before. We watched almost every game from the first round in late April to the championship game in early June—Adam and I, with the enormous Winston leaning heavily against Adam's leg and the golden Sadie sleeping either in Winston's bed or under Adam's outstretched arm. Sometimes he sat on the floor with Winston, haunch to haunch, in uncomplicated friendship. He often wore a pair of odd, khaki-colored pants, not chinos and not sweats, but with a drawstring at the waist, and a cheap, thin sweatshirt with a hood. Every sound in the lower level was muffled, as it was in the treatment room at Duke.

We could hear Jenny puttering around or vacuuming upstairs in another universe; occasionally she would appear with two cups of tea. We occasionally conferred about the finer points of the game or any other matter he wanted to discuss, but mostly these were quiet mornings.

The only good laughs we enjoyed were connected with his big dog Winston. Once, when a noise from the bathroom startled me, I jumped and said, "What . . . ?"

"That would be Winston, pushing up the toilet seat."

I worried out loud about a newborn baby sharing a house with a Great Dane. Adam knew that I am phobic when it comes to dogs or at least uncomfortable in their presence. He seemed to delight in my disapproval when I said, "You don't *know* this dog. You don't know his psychiatric history. Look at the size of those jaws."

One morning when I was sitting in the den, Winston ambled over to greet me, his big head and teeth inches from my face, a great stalactite of slobber exactly at my eye level. In mock horror Adam said, "Dad, for the love of *God,* no sudden movements. *Please!"*

When the play-offs were over we silently wondered how we would fill up the time between us, until we realized the Tour de France would see us through the next few weeks. After the Tour there would be nothing.

Jenny's mom and dad came up from Charlotte regularly. Jim, an architect, took time away from his practice to work in the yard and do repairs around the house, while Alice helped Jenny get ready for the baby. Sarah and her husband, Paul, were there a lot too, to support Jenny and to keep Adam company. Paul assembled the baby's crib and did carpentry work in her alcove. Alice said to Tracy, "The four of us sit in that room downstairs, playing Scrabble at two o'clock in the afternoon on a workday, and pretend it's normal."

Occasionally, Adam's old friend Jason Harrod stopped by to visit and mow the grass. When they were in high school, he and Adam had spent many hours picking and strumming, singing, and Adam playing his harmonica, too. Jason had gone on to a successful career in music, performing and recording his own ballads in a raspy, sweet southern voice. Sometimes he sang to Adam. We would hear him again.

Adam dedicated a part of each day to reading the Bible. He had always been interested in the Bible, but now he was reading it the way Jacob wrestled with the angel. And, like Jacob, he refused to let it go without a blessing. Adam and Jenny read the Bible by voicing it aloud to one another, like actors reading for a part or lectors at Evening Prayer. As they worked their way through a passage they took frequent breaks to discuss its meaning and to pray about its themes. Like most of Adam's conversations, his Bible reading had a vocational focus: what shall we make of my dying? He was forever trying to find two characters in the sacred text named Adam and Jenny. And what if one of them is, say, *dying* and the other one is, let's say, *pregnant*? They read the Bible passionately, as the poet Adrienne Rich urged in any act of reading—"Read," she said, "as if your life depended on it."

They didn't plunder the Bible for easy answers but treated it as a book of hard questions. They believed that even the most obscure passage will yield a grace to those who respectfully seek it. In the Gospel of Mark, for example, why does Jesus turn away the foreign woman who seeks his help (*and, God forbid, is he turning away from me*)? What is the use of prayer (*when the answer is always No*)? How can I take up my cross and follow Jesus (*in my condition—or does my condition count as a cross*)? What exactly is heaven (*and how shall we love one another there*)?

He and I passed the mornings watching basketball, sometimes on *mute,* so we could talk, but never disagree, about matters of faith. At first, I missed our old combativeness and the days when he would say, "But *Dad,* that's not an argument." He had begun to treat me as a venerable theologian, even as he raised questions no honest theologian could answer with certainty.

When we talked about sickness, death, and eternal life, Adam approached those topics both with the confidence of a believer and the wrinkled brow of a seeker. He was like a man driving in the fog: he is certain there is a road out there and a way forward, but his headlights will only go so far. He complained to Tom Colley, our Lutheran pastor at St. Paul's, that he never heard a preacher who was willing to admit, "I don't know." When he finally found one, it was only his dad.

"So, why did Jesus heal so many people in Galilee, and why so few in North Carolina?"

I said, "In my opinion, the healings weren't intended as medical cures for us to duplicate. Think of all the lepers who just missed him when he passed through Capernaum, or the mothers in all the villages around Nain who had to bury their children. The miracles are like flares calling attention to the glory of God. They're signs of the great redemption to come.

I'm like you. I still find the meaning of God in the cross and not the miracles."

"Maybe so," he said, touching his own cross, but like a patient who is contemplating a second opinion.

Our discussions were marked by a deepening irony. It was an awkward dance we did through the summer of 2005. He deferred to my knowledge, while I secretly envied his faith. We quietly reversed our roles, and that reversal would continue without our acknowledging it, and continues still.

When it came to the spiritual life, Adam and I were moving in opposite directions. His faith was in the ascendancy, mine was losing ground; he was climbing Jacob's Ladder, I was sinking down. He had been seized by certainties about God that I couldn't match. He relied on individual verses of the Bible and found security in them as I had never done. He read Scripture the way a lawyer combs through the fine print of statutory law and then stakes his case on it.

Just as Adam was mastering the discipline of prayer, I was losing my ability to pray. I didn't stop praying in anger but in something nearer to fatigue; it was an emptiness so complete that I couldn't remember what it was to be full. No shaking of the fist toward heaven and no dark night of the soul for me, at least, none that I was conscious of. It wasn't that I quit believing in God, only that I had apparently misunderstood the scope of God's responsibilities, the way a citizen might telephone the Department of Finance to complain about a broken water main when everyone knows, or should know, that the Department of Finance *never* fixes broken water mains. It was my mistake, not God's fault. I simply took away the prayer book and candle from the little cabinet shrine in my study, where I had spent many hours telephoning God about Adam, and replaced them with an unabridged dictionary.

Adam became my altar, and on him I laid my every offering. His spirit was approaching perfection, while everything but love for him was drying up in me. Oddly, that didn't stop me from encouraging his faith or being glad for it, even though I was running on habits of speech rather than conviction. I was following the writer Georges Bernanos' advice: "If you can't pray—at least say your prayers."

The same raveled love produced a little cancer dance among us in the summer of 2005—not uncommon among the dying and members of their family, who want nothing more than to shield one another from the sorrow each is experiencing, who wish to pretend that no one is dying, desperate, or cut to the heart. In this dance the patient always leads, the loved ones follow. The basic step is simple enough: embrace the love but hold those who offer it at arm's length from your pain. A tango with the terminally ill.

Why this dance? Because with cancer some sort of physical overexposure—it doesn't deserve to be called "intimacy"—becomes a daily occurrence, and it's disgusting. Wounds, night sweats, vomit, and horrible constipation—all of it must be cleansed, laundered, scrubbed, and suffered. If there's any dignity left, it won't occur in the body but in the patient's emotional life, where boundaries still count for something.

Father David told me that caregivers should "lean in"

to another's pain but keep their own feet on the ground and maintain their own center of gravity. Parents are not very good at that. Parents don't lean but lunge headlong into the child's suffering. Immersed in their own heartache, they can barely function on behalf of their child.

Adam decided to spare himself the added burden of two ruined parents. He relied on their love, but he didn't need their emotional collapse as its proof. He didn't want to see his father or his mother cry. Adam will accept the tears of his sister Sarah but not those of his parents. Weeping is out.

If there is a method to this rule, it is poignantly captured by William Stafford in an ode to his dead son:

> *You turned once to tell me something,*
> *But then you glimpsed a shadow on my face*
> *And maybe thought, Why tell what hurts?*
> *You carried it, my boy, so brave, so far.*

The child cannot tolerate the grief of his parents because it is damp with memory. They grieve not merely the young man who stands before them, but also the boy with his cocker spaniel, the nervous teenager on his first date, and the homesick college student. As they watch him move haltingly across the room, they are remembering a high-stepping drum major with brass buttons on his chest. The grown child becomes a transparency for a lifetime of memories. The wise young man avoids this role like the plague. After a lengthy process of separation from mom and dad, the last thing the child wants is to be reinserted into the sticky old nucleus. The Past is out.

The parents have lived long enough to know what an

empty future looks like. They desperately hope the child is too unimaginative to have glimpsed it or that he has somehow failed to value his own youth. One day, a friend of Adam's said to me, "You knew he expected to live until Christmas. . . ." Well, no, as a matter of fact, I did not know that. That is a piece of information I could have done without. I had hoped that when my son proclaimed, "Time is irrelevant," he had forgotten how to tell time. Make-believe is out.

Adam, the beloved tyrant:

He will brook no excessive displays of affection. If the usual adult greeting is a hug of moderate intensity and a single kiss on his massive forehead, let all greetings follow the same pattern. He alone is permitted to break this rule. Clinging is out.

He will authorize no unsupervised parental conversations with his treatment nurse. He is in charge of his own illness and will handle it on his terms and no one else's. Interfering is out.

The father-to-be will entertain no parental wisdom on the subject of caring for a newborn or raising a child. He has read books and attended classes on these subjects. Although the birth of his daughter lies three months in the future, the entire experience already belongs to him as if it had been deposited to his account. Advising is out.

So they dance, as if on the ledge of a tall building, two parents and their adult child. They must avoid missteps in the form of pity, pathos, or emotional overreaching of any kind. They must not impose their meaning on the dance or over-interpret it. Leaning is permitted, lunging is out.

But most of all, they must keep dancing—and *never* look down.

The cancer dance, along with the other little fictions and dis-honesties that attend a terminal illness, would have been unen-durable, were it not for the table and the common meal, where we could laugh, pray, relax, and be our true selves. If his dying made us a little weird, eating made us human again.

On many evenings Adam and Jenny came to our house for dinner. Since Tracy's mother, Nina, was a patient in the medi-cal wing of a nearby convalescent center, we had reason to gather our extended family as often as possible. Tracy's brother, Regan, and his wife, Mary, came down frequently from New Jersey, and their daughter, Moriah, dropped by from UNC in Chapel Hill. Other cousins and friends of Adam flew in from St. Louis and New York and Houston. Our Sarah and Paul along with four-year-old Luke and baby Calvin were always at home with us, making weekly visits from Charlottesville even as the family was packing up to move to Winston-Salem. Tracy's father, Bob, who had moved into the convalescent center to be near Nina, was usually willing to leave her side for brief excursions to our table.

Each member of the family had a designated place at the table. I was seated at one end with my back to a triple window that opens onto a small garden with grasses and flowers. Under normal circumstances Tracy would have sat at the other end of the table for easy access to the kitchen. But since Adam was the reason for the feast, it was only right that he should sit in Tracy's place at the head of the table. He became our absurdly young patriarch and presiding guest. He rarely missed a meal even when he couldn't eat.

These were not somber gatherings. Often, before we ate in the dining area, Sarah, Adam, Paul, and Jenny played cards or told old stories in the breakfast room beside the kitchen.

"Do you remember when we discovered Dad was a plagiarist?"

Adam knows the answer: "*Oliver Twist*—hell, we should have known he didn't make that stuff up."

"That caused quite a *brouhaha,*" she replies, testing her brother's memory of another issue. "He never wrote vocabulary words on *my* lunch bag every day," she adds. "But I did love that word 'brouhaha.'"

"Don't *patronize* me," Adam says, and for a moment he is Little Brother again, respectful of his older sister's learning but wearied by yet another of his father's hated vocabulary words.

I would lead the prayers before supper. Sometimes we simply recited the German table grace, "Come Lord Jesus," *Komm, Herr Jesu,* but more often than not we gave thanks for food and family and asked a special blessing for Adam and Nina, concluding with a sentence from the liturgy, "Grace our table with your presence, and give us a foretaste of the feast to come."

It was my job to pray. Apparently, I attended four years of seminary and received an advanced degree in theology for the sole purpose of praying at all meals and family occasions. I have tenure in this role. But despite my training I am not fluent in prayer, and my prayers tend to be overly pious and unimaginative. One evening I said, "Let us pray" (sounding too much like a clergyman, perhaps), and from the other end of the table I heard the guest of honor say, "Tee it up, big guy."

. . .

One afternoon, two of my divinity students appeared at our door. They were young men in their early twenties, unmarried, each toting platters and bowls of cooked food, like Christmas presents. Having driven up the professor's long driveway and knocked on his door unannounced, they were a little nervous but still certain of what they needed to do. One of them carried an enormous baked ham covered with glazed fruit—and not merely pineapple slices, but cherries, currants, apricots, and plums. On his forearm he balanced a shopping bag filled with homemade rolls. The other fellow had a spinach soufflé in the flat of one hand, and scalloped potatoes, browned on the top and crisp-looking, in the other. He had laid potholders in both hands to protect his palms.

After we put the food in the kitchen we sat quietly for a few minutes in the living room. No one knew what to say, but their gifts had removed any awkwardness from the silence. Finally, I said, "You two are such accomplished cooks, I should say, chefs. Are these your recipes?" They looked at one another and actually blushed, then replied virtually in unison, "I called my mom."

From mid-April to the autumn of 2005 we cooked almost nothing. When we thanked God for food, we were actually giving thanks for the friends, students, and generous strangers who delivered prepared meals to our house (and Jenny and Adam's) virtually every day of the week. Our caterers were colleagues from the Divinity School, parishioners from Immaculate Conception, and lawyers from Durham and Chapel Hill. Often our friends brought meals we had shared in their home during better days, and sometimes they stayed and joined us for dinner. Some of the people we hardly knew, including the women of Mount Level Baptist Church, where one of my colleagues is the pastor, who sent over fried chicken, black-eyed peas, and corn bread. One day a lawyer from Chapel Hill showed up with 140 frozen meatballs.

That summer we arrived at the most basic level of dependency, that of receiving nourishment from the hands of others. The entire season was a single blurred meal. The Divinity School's contributions were the result of an effort organized by my colleagues Teresa Berger and Mary Fulkerson, but the real benefit was the human contact and gestures of love we were learning to accept. Many were offering their key-signature meals. Our entire family learned not to be absent for Ellen's Moroccan chicken, Bill and Mary's flank steak smothered in onions, or Mal's Russian cream cake. We got hooked on Jenny Copeland's peach cobbler made exclusively from *Upstate* South Carolina peaches. She was our Cobbler Queen. It's almost embarrassing to remember how often, in the midst of the most somber of situations, our thoughts would turn to food. Sitting in a depressing blood lab or treatment room, one of us would break the silence: "Who's coming tonight?" "I wonder if they'll do the broccoli-and-cheddar thing with the bread crumbs."

Adam and Jenny usually ate the least and left earliest because they were in a hurry to get home and to get on with their rituals. At the end of the day they would retreat up the open-tread stairs to their tree-house bedroom. Their hideaway had become no less a sanctuary than the Daily Mass Chapel at Immaculate Conception. From the alcove beside their bedroom they could look down into their living room or upward to a tiny deck perched like a gondola at the peak of the house. The alcove was already expecting a baby. It was decorated with a mobile with ducks and bears and a child's dresser.

First they watched a movie, Jenny told me, usually a romantic comedy or a political thriller. If the film had a cynical or violent side, they turned it off.

After the movie, Jenny lit the candles again and they read a portion of the Bible aloud. Then they recited a psalm or a verse from the Lutheran *Order of Vespers:*

> *Let my prayers be set forth before you as incense,*
> *And the lifting up of my hands as the evening sacrifice.*

Sometimes they read from *A Private House of Prayer,* compiled by the spiritual writer Leslie Weatherhead. The book is loosely modeled after Teresa of Ávila's *The Interior Castle.* The spiritual life is organized into seven rooms, the last of which Weatherhead describes as "a big room at the top of the house," which in my mind corresponded to Adam and Jenny's bedroom.

Adam told me they prayed the psalms most nights, and I understand why. The psalms are filled with the complexities of rage, and so was Adam. It is never pure anger at work in any of us, and it wasn't in him, but anger in the disguises and permutations of fear, suffering, sadness, and bafflement. The psalms are filled with questions; they ask "why?" and "how long?" Sometimes they address God disrespectfully in a manner that good religious people find offensive. But they also offer more than the usual, therapeutic alternatives of suppressing the rage or projecting it onto others. They invite the believer to lay the whole mess before God. The psalms treat God as a partner in suffering and in doing so they open a narrow path from lament to a grudging acknowledgment of God's love. In the psalms Adam and Jenny found a script for moving from their worst fears to a powerful affirmation of trust. From the resentful, "Hear my voice, O God, in my complaint" to the joyful, "Hope in God; for I shall again praise him."

The psalms were important to Adam and Jenny because medical science is deaf to suffering. It responds to pain when it can be connected to a physical problem and quantified. "On a scale of one to ten, how would you rate your pain?" But suffering, with its many depths and its mysterious interplay of body and spirit, is beyond the scope of pain and therefore beyond the competence of most medical practitioners. There were times when Adam wanted to tell somebody about his sadness, fear, or anger, but the hospital provided no acoustic space for that kind of talk.

What must not under any circumstances be uttered in the clinic may be shouted from the rooftop of any church, synagogue, or candlelit bedroom, even if it is a prayer addressed to the very One who has abandoned you:

My God, my God, why have you
  forsaken me?

Why are you so far from
   helping me, from the
   words of my groaning?
O my God, I cry by day, but you
   do not answer;
   and by night, but find no rest.

When they are finished with praying (as I imagine the scene), he pats his wife's belly and, using her secret name, says good night to the baby.

Then Jenny blows out the candles in their sanctuary at the top of the house and the darkness surrounds them with its own natural gifts.

They sleep.

When the sun comes up it will be time again for the Flor Essence Tea, scented candles, and his anointing at the hands of a pregnant girl in shorts and a t-shirt. As Jenny stands next to the bed or kneels beside him, he will greet the baby with the morning's kiss, and their summer ritual will begin anew.

II

May was our month for coming to terms with the shocking cruelties of April. The air grew heavy and warm, and the first colors since autumn made a brief appearance along the outcroppings of limestone behind the house. The few plantings the deer refused to eat—the daffodils, chrysanthemum, abelia, and the enormous butterfly bush beside the garage—had either gone or were fading fast. With the coming of the heat there would be no going back to early mornings with a nip in the air or to leisurely rains that made the flowers in the meadow smell like Easter. We were about to trade the promise of spring for the blister of a Carolina summer.

Adam's treatments continued as he and Jenny settled into their deepening life of prayer and devotion. For our part, we treated ourselves to a little springtime hope that his regimen of radiation and chemotherapy might be working to good effect.

On their sixth wedding anniversary Jenny and Adam went

to dinner at the Top of the Hill in Chapel Hill. The next day he unveiled a revised approach to fighting his disease. Like a diplomat announcing a new initiative, he informed us that we would confront his cancer as a team, and the four of us—Adam, Jenny, Tracy, and I—would do everything medical together. We would make a foursome for every treatment, inoculation, consultation, and scan. He had t-shirts made with the words TEAM ADAM on them, which none of us could ever bear to put on except for Tracy who occasionally slept in hers.

His new plan only confirmed our family's practice from the beginning, but by announcing it as "policy" he injected the derring-do of hope and a little drama into the routines of cancer treatment. Perhaps he had learned something from the best of his childhood doctors, who always had a Plan B, and then a Plan C and D, each of which they projected with such decisiveness that we virtually forgot that everything after Plan A was a shot in the dark. The trick, of course, was never to run out of letters.

The t-shirts made me sad; but then everything was making me sad. I dragged myself to our school's baccalaureate service expecting only the annual formulary in which gowned professors file into the gothic chapel, sit in the same seats year after year, and observe the interminable ceremony of hooding. Even in a good year, one counts the minutes. But when you are being crushed by sadness, the very last thing you need is the enthusiasm of divinity graduates and the rhetoric of new beginnings. The service promised everything to the students and their proud families, but nothing to me.

It was the Saturday night before Pentecost, the Christian festival of the Holy Spirit. The altar and pulpit were dressed in red. From the lectern one of the students read from the prophet:

> *"I will pour out my Spirit*
> *on all flesh;*
> *your sons and your daughters*
> *shall prophesy,*
> *your old men shall dream dreams*
> *and your young men shall*
> *see visions."*

No doubt our young graduates had visions of a bright future in ministry, but for this old man the night was made for dreaming. I could only dream for Adam and our family and all who suffer. From the Gospel that evening Jesus spoke to my true condition: "Let anyone who is thirsty come to me. . . ."

I don't remember anything of the sermon or the service except for the waterfall of a thousand voices singing "Be Thou My Vision."

> *Great God of heaven, my victory won,*
> *may I reach heaven's joys, O bright heaven's Sun!*
> *Heart of my own heart, whatever befall,*
> *still be my vision, O Ruler of all.*

I came home that evening buoyed by something new and unexpected. It was the same sense of lift Adam must have felt when he had the t-shirts made. Until that time I was completely ignorant of hope, perhaps because I had never been so desperately in need of it. But that night I momentarily lost my fear of hope, which is nothing other than the fear of death, and remembered again the Bible's quaint promise, "Hope maketh not ashamed." *I will not be ashamed of my hope.* When this new thing took over in me it was like nothing I had ever felt; for as long as I had it I was unnaturally energized, like the ninety-pound weakling who with a rush of adrenaline manages to lift a car off the accident victim. It wasn't that I believed Adam would be cured, but in defiance of all the evidence I was positive he would survive and our family would remain whole.

For reasons I can't explain, I don't regret the hope. I would never delete it from the spring of 2005 or from the larger human repertoire. But, Team Adam notwithstanding, his medical treatment proved a disappointing story. He bravely followed his schedule of treatments, but they never yielded a decent plot with a rising and falling action or a dramatic turning point. The curtain was never raised on much of anything and therefore it never fell. Whatever was going on in his body missed its appointment with our hope. They never met. One day, as we left a meeting with the oncologist, Jenny said, "It's never good news, is it."

And even if we dared to hope, there was always the radiology report. Adam had unwisely asked for a printout, and the radiologist on duty had unwisely given it to him, as if the patient's right to know includes the right to thumb through his own death warrant. It was one thing to hear "small tumors on the side" and "spots on the liver" or even the radiologist's spoken verdict, "incurable," delivered to Adam and Jenny with utensil-like efficiency. It was quite another to see it in black and white. In addition to finding "dramatic" progression in the thoracic region, brain, and liver, the report counted up the bones from his clavicle to his pelvis in which the cancer had also appeared. Adam and Jenny read the document soberly word by word. Then they treated it in the only way possible, as a contaminant that must not remain in their home. One day in May, Adam gave it to me.

Tracy and I did feel something like hope after meeting with another Duke oncologist who specialized in primary brain tumors (Adam's was metastatic). He was everything Adam's primary doctor was not: brash, abrupt, sure of his genius, but less polished in his speech. He was also older, with a record of astonishing successes. A colleague referred us to him for a second opinion with the ultimate recommendation: "He's been on *60 Minutes*." He projected just the mix of confidence and compassion we were looking for. On his card, where one would have expected professional titles and degrees, he had printed in boldface type words we were desperate to hear: THERE IS HOPE.

He was furious with Tracy and me for coming for our first meeting without Adam and threatened to walk out of the room. He had agreed to see us only because we were a part of the "Duke family." We tried to explain that Adam had asked us to make the initial contact, that he was exhausted by probes and tests, and that we simply wanted the doctor to respond to the scans he had before him on the table. Team Adam promised never to come again without its namesake.

There was hope, he said in a deeply resonant and commanding voice. "Your son is not dead yet." Adam should follow the reasonable course of treatments set before him by his primary oncologist. "If they fail," he said with the decisiveness we craved, "we still have some other things we can do." I tucked his card into my breast pocket, and we left more encouraged than we had been in three weeks.

The lull between Adam's first and second round of treatments offered the cruelest hope of all. Just as we began to accept him as a cancer patient whose color and energy were depleted and who occasionally threw up after a sip of ginger ale, he got it all back between treatments, including something of the natural light behind his eyes. Suddenly, he was a handsome, tousle-haired young man again who moved gracefully from room to room instead of lumbering about and lying on the couch. He was laughing and playing cards with his sister and brother-in-law; he referred to his blooming, beautiful wife as "hot," making her blush in front of the whole family. We found ourselves recycling through the stages of grief, tarrying this time in the denial stage. "He doesn't look sick," we said almost as a reproach.

The entries in my diary in early May reflect the battle between hope and pessimism as well as the more bizarre juxtaposition of death and the mundane. We were living a double life, suspended between the routines of ordinary spring days and the eternal weight of glory hidden within them. As we waited for developments in Adam, Nina, Jenny, and the baby, and with the heat bearing down on us, we had stumbled onto the fullness of time.

A diary entry on May 1 reads, "12:15 healing" to remind me of a brief liturgy of anointing after church. Monday through Friday Adam received his poisons; on Sunday, along with six or seven others, he would be anointed with oil. Oil and poison. The oil was not intended to counteract the chemicals in his system but to signify the healing that was possible even in the presence of poison.

Only two days later I note the discovery of a small inpatient facility in nearby Hillsborough located in a pleasant setting and surrounded by trees. It is a hospice.

On May 4, a baby shower has been scheduled for Jenny at Tracy's law office. We have a photo of Adam holding up one of the gifts, a tiny pink jumper. He is wearing an olive drab shirt with long graceful sleeves. His hair is soft and parted neatly in the middle. His face bears the same quizzical smile that would later become his trademark, but now his cane is visible against the wall behind him.

On May 6 a telephone message from William Sloane Coffin invites me to call him whenever I need to. Coffin and I had corresponded off and on in recent years, but I was only a seminarian when he became famous for his antiwar activities at Yale, and we had never met. I was not a "friend of Bill" and felt more comfortable calling him "Reverend Coffin." Yet he was willing to deal pastorally with me, which meant he was not afraid to talk to me about the death of my son—as well as the death of his son, Alexander, who had died twenty-two years earlier.

There are other, more mundane notations, most of which have been scratched over: May 5, "senior banquet," crossed off. May 8, a university meeting I was obliged to attend, crossed off. "Barberry bushes planted," incredibly, not crossed off but planted and still growing. An outing to a Durham Bulls baseball game arranged by a few of my students who thought it would be just what I needed, crossed off.

While our son was wrestling with death, I managed to plant shrubbery, buy a shirt, have the printer repaired, and work out. I made an index to a small book I had written the year before.

I think of my mother who had her hair done religiously even as she was dying of congestive heart failure, or of a neighbor who washed his car every Friday while he wasted away with cancer. What exactly is the significance of having your hair done, washing your car, or planting a few barberry bushes in the face of death?

On May 25 my diary says, "Change dedication." The little book I had written was a revision of some lectures I had given at Yale the year Adam and Jenny were married. Adam had immediately sensed the importance of these lectures to me and took a few days off work to join Tracy and me in New Haven. Before we went up to Yale we spent the weekend in New York City with our New Jersey relatives and friends. We enjoyed a family dinner reminiscent of his graduation party and then walked a few blocks to Lincoln Center for a performance of *Madama Butterfly*. The next morning, with a light rain falling on the city, the three of us grabbed some bagels and caught the train to New Haven.

Even then, I knew enough to be thankful that Adam was

with us for these days. There was never a question that the book, if it ever got written, would be dedicated to him. Now with the manuscript in its final proofs, I felt the need to make one last change.

At the last possible moment, I added these words to the dedication:

> *They shall mount up with wings as eagles;*
> *they shall run, and not be weary.*

They are taken from one of the prophet Isaiah's images of the restoration of Israel and the renewal of the entire human family. I'm sure I was not thinking so much of the children of Israel when I wrote them as of my own child Adam, heavily medicated and sunk in his recliner when he should have been out playing tennis or running with the dogs.

Late one evening in the third week in May, Tracy's mother, Nina, died. For days she had lain in a darkened room near her husband Bob's room on the residential wing of the convalescent center. The health of Tracy's parents had been our chief preoccupation until Adam was diagnosed with a recurrence of cancer. Then we began our shuttle from grief to grief, each with its own character of sadness. Bob was focused on Nina and yet sorrowing for Adam. Tracy and I were consumed by Adam's illness yet burdened by Nina's and worried about Bob. Jenny was living for Adam and the baby but concerned for her mother, Alice, who had just been diagnosed with breast cancer. Sarah was living at a distance in Charlottesville, caring for a newborn baby and heartsick for her brother. Everyone in our family was grieving but in a slightly different key.

After her mother died, Tracy sat alone with the body for more than an hour before bringing her father to our house for the night. It was about twelve-thirty or one o'clock in the morning, and the three of us were sitting in the dimly lit break-fast room quietly drinking tea, when the phone rang. It was a woman from the funeral home who called to say, "I want you to know we have your mother's body and we are caring for it." That was it. Only two hours earlier, as we brooded over Nina, we had said of her corpse—somewhat defensively—"That's not Nina." But now this stranger's voice in the middle of the night said only, "We have your mother—her body," and we were comforted in a way we could not have explained.

Adam's illness had separated him from his beloved grand-mother. Fear of infection played a role in that separation, but also the pathos of their mutual suffering was more than either of them could bear. Whenever Tracy broached the subject of Adam to Nina, her mother's face would collapse in despair as if she were hearing the news of his illness for the first time. When Nina's name was mentioned in Adam's presence, he would grow sullen and withdraw from the conversation. Perhaps they were thinking of a photograph in our home, revealing a beautiful young grandmother and a towheaded, white-blond boy in a Duke t-shirt. They are both wearing short shorts, lolling on a dune at the beach, he with his head against her shoulder and a stalk of sea grass in his mouth. Adam and Nina resorted to speaking on the telephone and finally sending each other messages as if they were prisoners on separate cellblocks.

We carried the messages back and forth, as did our minister Tom Colley, who offered himself as a pastor and confessor to Nina. Nina was a believer who hadn't attended church in a long time, but with Tom's help she had begun to seek in earnest what she had always possessed.

Nina had an unerring nose for religious hypocrisy, which might have explained her problem with "good Christian people." Once when one of her high school history students regaled the whole class with his father's pious judgment of the Jews, Nina gave him an assignment to go home and remind his father that Jesus was a Jew. "And that goes for his disciples, too—*and* his mother." She did not suffer fools gladly. One day a former student came up to her on the street and said, "Hello, Doc, you don't remember me, do you?" Nina, who had a PhD in history and had accumulated three decades' worth of students, replied, "No, I don't. I didn't have any bald, middle-aged men in my classes." Before she lapsed into her final sleep, she was giving family counseling to her caregivers in the convalescent center. One of them, a middle-aged woman struggling with rebellious teenagers and an indifferent husband, brought her whole family to Nina's bedside for a pep talk. All Nina the historian asked from me was a large map of the world, which I pinned to the wall where she could see it from her bed.

We took turns sitting in the dark with Nina as she slept. Her room was dominated by an enormous bullet-shaped tank of oxygen beside her bed. In the evening hours it seemed to grow larger and hiss louder. I began to think of it as "Little Boy" and to worry that it would explode. In one of my dreams the tank *does* explode. It was not filled with oxygen, but blood.

I was trying to concentrate on Nina, but in my grief for her I kept seeing Adam's face superimposed on hers. She had become the first act in a tragedy yet to reach its climax. I began to wonder if Adam would die like this, in a dark room amidst the sounds of air leaking from an oxygen bomb.

In those days the most resilient person in our family was my wife. She was witnessing the slow, painful death of the one who had borne her and the approaching death of the one she had borne. It must have felt to her that two struggles were grinding on in her own body. She was also caring for her father, supporting Jenny, comforting Sarah, and holding me close to her at night. When I think of Tracy in the summer of 2005, a comment by Kathleen Norris in *The Cloister Walk* rings true: "One of the most astonishing and precious things about motherhood is the brave way in which women consent to give birth to creatures who will one day die."

A few nights before she died, Nina had a vision that she reported to Tracy and Tracy reported to me. Unlike most events of this nature, Nina's did not occur after a sudden trauma, but toward the end of a long sleep. This is what she said:

"I'm in heaven."

"Is it nice, Momma?"

"It's *heaven,*" she replied, incredulous at the question. "It's not like here. All the *lights* are on. Don't you know, it's *heaven.*"

The only possible sequel to such testimony is death itself.

A portion of Nina's ashes was interred among the trees surrounding Saint Paul's columbarium. The brief service was conducted against the backdrop of a semicircular wall containing the names and ashes of the dead in our parish. Nina and Bob had not lived in our city or attended our church, and therefore we had no expectations of a congregation. When our family entered the bower-like place of worship I was surprised to see scores of friends, members of the church, her doctor from Duke, and nurses from the convalescent center standing in an arc behind the chairs, as if to enclose us and complete the circle begun by the wall.

The last persons to be seated were Adam and Jenny. I could sense everyone's eyes following them as they slowly made their way to their chairs. Jenny's pregnancy was clearly showing, as was Adam's worsening condition. No one could miss the contest between life and death that was raging in their bodies.

In that moment I felt surrounded by those who had loved and supported us our whole lives. It was as if the gathering of mourners had grown to include our family's blessed dead and those of every church we'd ever known, including the country people in our first congregation where Adam was baptized. They prayed for him the day he was born and watched him grow until he could stand on the tombstones and sing like a thrush. I could see the old men who trimmed the graves in their neatly pressed overalls, and their wives who taught Tracy how to make a garden and can vegetables. They all live in the cemetery now, hidden in the cleft of the hill behind the church. But for one day, today, they came out of their places in the earth and joined us for this solemn liturgy.

With everyone present and accounted for, the circle gently closed around Adam and Jenny and the rest of our family, and Nina's service began.

In his funeral homily Tom credited her growth in faith to the example of her grandson Adam and quoted a fragment of her confession: "If I am God's child, then, well, O Tom Colley, I see. I *see!*"

After the sermon, the pastor knelt beside some shrubbery and flowers and tenderly mixed a portion of Nina into the dirt, kneaded the mixture like dough, and covered her over.

Adam's condition visibly worsened during the succeeding rounds of whole-brain radiation and chemotherapy. The pain in his side and bones was wearing him down, and he was relying on enormous doses of OxyContin to keep up his daily routine. His instinct was to move like a graceful, lanky boy, but the cancer and his medications had caused him to trade his usual fluidity for the ponderousness of an older man. I had seen him affect deliberateness in a courtroom, leaning on a table, his hands splayed in reflection, but now he had it for real.

His hair was going when he decided to have his head shaved. I went with him to the barbershop, but he asked me to wait in the car for him. When he came out, I realized that one of my first nightmare images of my son as a bald cancer patient had just come true. I took a good look at him and mentally compared my fear with the reality. There he was, sitting next to me in the car, and the world had not changed. It felt like a triumph.

At first, he was indistinguishable from the company of smooth-headed men found in any coffee shop or on any basketball court. I once cruised through the Mad Hatter, one of our favorite watering holes, looking for Adam, and before I found him my eye fell on half a dozen young men who looked just like him. Gradually, this small comfort went away, as he grew to look less like a young cyclist stopping for an iced cappuccino and more like a young man of sorrows, and acquainted with grief, the sort you wish you could walk on all sides of at once in order to shield him from the casual double takes of strangers.

Small tumors appeared on the surface of his side and chest, at first only one or two, then several more. They did not hurt, but he was vexed by them and by the doctors' lack of interest in them.

If Adam trusted you, he would pull up his shirt and show them to you, the way I am told children with leukemia are not embarrassed to display their bruises to others. Once, during a visit with our pastor Tom Colley, Adam showed him his tumors, and Tom had the good sense to know he had just been received as a pastor. On one occasion, we were with Adam in an examination room and he pulled up his shirt to reveal six or eight tumors which he had carefully circled with a green magic marker, as if they were significant passages he had underlined in his prayer book. It was his way of saying, Try to ignore these; I dare you. When he bared his chest he was baring his soul, but the resident, knowing that the action was in the brain, ignored them without so much as a word.

After his fourth round of chemotherapy with no good response to point to, Adam was still thinking about the future.

There was a life to be lived with Jenny and his daughter. To have listened to him one would have thought he was at the headwaters of his treatment. We were back in Clinic 2 K again, and he was reclining on the same high examination table, propped on one elbow with his back against the wall just as he had been on April 13. But by now he had lost some weight and color, his eyes had darkened, and he was using a cane. When the doctor gently included stopping all treatments on his list of options, Adam said to the room and to no one in particular, "I haven't been tested yet."

It was early June when his doctor confirmed our fears. The latest scans showed the combination of radiation and Temodar had done nothing. The cancer was growing. We were more than willing to *mis*understand his interpretation of the radiology reports. We were only too happy to hear what we wanted to hear. Tracy said, "You mean the four lesions in the brain have grown in size?"

"No," the oncologist replied forcefully. Then he made himself clear with a word Tracy, Jenny, and I have seared in our common memory. "They are innumerable."

The only "innumerable" I had ever visualized was an infinity of blessings—which the Bible compares to stars, grains of sand, and the aeons of God's eternity.

With this new iteration of the multitude, something like fatigue settled into the room. We made no sudden movements or changes of expression because we had no energy to do so. The doctor went on for a few minutes as we sat there vacantly like commuters on a train. When he was finished, we gathered our notepads and purses and the list of questions we had brought with us and left the clinic.

I recently came across the yellow legal pad on which Tracy took a few scattered and disorganized notes on the conference, including the names of the next drugs to be tried. At the bottom of the page she has scrawled a single word: "Innumerable."

12

It is a blistering Tuesday in June, and Adam is on something of a shopping spree. We are moving ever so slowly through the newest and grandest of our city's malls, inching our way across its broad promenade past the chain stores and eateries, ascending and descending its three sets of escalators.

Today, we will visit the eight jewelry stores spread throughout the mall. His diligence reminds me of the man in Jesus' parable who is seeking the pearl of great price, but this afternoon it's a bracelet we're after.

We have it down to two, one in silver, another in 14-karat gold. The first allows for charms, the second is fancy. The first is a little plain and clunky, too large for a slender wrist; the other is filigreed and delicate, too old-fashioned for a teenager.

The clerks are mostly women who know him and greet him warmly. He enters each shop with the assured air of a regular, and a high roller at that. Last week he was trolling for diamonds with Tracy; he bought an expensive piece for Jenny and had it gift wrapped in silver foil with white ribbons and bows. The women in the stores must wonder what he is up to. Some of them know.

We have come back to the first store, where the clerk has not waited on him before and doesn't seem to know him. She is heavily made up and her hair is dark and perfect. She glistens with store product. She gives away her age by the size of her glasses, which are saucers with burgundy rims.

She is not the ideal person to wait on my son, who for all his shopping experience is lacking jewelry store etiquette. When he examines a bracelet he does not first compliment it with "Oh, *that's* nice," but simply studies it like a rabbi poring over the Masoretic text. It has been this way in every store. He has felt, fingered, and rotated against the light every bracelet in the entire mall and perhaps in the entire city and surrounding county.

When she pulls some other merchandise out of a drawer, he asks, "Where did you get those? Aren't they good enough to display?" She is growing impatient with his manner and his rambling questions, and even more impatient with me for trying to smooth over his insensitivity with fatherly chuckles, as if my boy has just asked the cleverest question in the class.

She wants to know, "Is it for a special occasion?" expecting a description of the occasion but getting only "Yes."

"Does she wear a lot of jewelry?"

"Oh, yes," he answers confidently, as if he would know.

"The young people seem more comfortable with sterling silver these days. She might prefer silver to gold. What do you think?"

"That's hard to say," he replies, now realizing that he is over his head in this conversation. "I really don't know," he says, defeated.

She sighs, briefly gazes out into the mall at nothing in particular, then comes back to make her own careful assessment of Adam, looking not at his shaved head but into his eyes. It is a look that begins in annoyance and ends in revelation. Scales are falling from her saucer eyes. Under the fluorescent lights, something is thawing in her, and suddenly she *gets* it.

Still looking into Adam's eyes, she says softly, "I'm sure you know what she likes."

We take the silver. He politely treats my offer to buy a charm as a paternal tic and refuses. "You can't get this one," he says.

He is closing in on his goal of eighteen birthday gifts for his unborn daughter. Only two more to go. He chose a Duke cheerleader's outfit for her third. She will be adorable in it, sitting in the rafters of Cameron Indoor Stadium with her grandparents, doing the cheers and precision hand movements. Only we won't let her say, "Go to hell, Carolina / go to hell," or if we do, it will be our secret.

He has also bought a ceramic frog with a bubble-maker, a white cotton dress with ruffles and a bow for her seventh Easter, and fourteen other gifts.

Adam's pantry is almost full.

I am tempted to tell him that what he is doing is over the top. I want to warn him against trying to control eighteen years of the future, which is too much future for anyone to master, but I know how he will reply: "Oh, and why do you teach, if not to control the future? And why did you tell me what to do when I was a kid, if not . . ." So I tell Jenny instead, "His future is the child's sparkling DNA, her eyes that will dance like his, and her values that you and Adam share. They will all be hers, and he will always be with her."

But Jenny only replies, "It pleases him."

He no longer talks to me about the future, but he apparently still passionately believes in it. He is exercising his terminal imagination and taking great pleasure in mentally placing his child at the center of the scenes these gifts will create. He can see her sitting in the middle of a circle of children shredding the wrapping paper and bows and opening his gift.

What could be less grim than going to the mall and shopping for a little girl you love? Jenny tells me that when they shop for their daughter they are never sad, even though they know they are "pretending."

That same imagination was at work earlier in the week when he commissioned a dollhouse for her. He and Jenny had discovered our pastor Tom Colley's genius for building enormous model airplanes, ships, and his specialty: large, made-to-design, authentic-to-the-smallest-detail dollhouses. Adam and Jenny visited the craftsman in his workshop, an attached garage that resembled Geppetto's studio. Tom, Adam, and Jenny then nosed around our old house in Durham to take some photographs for Tom to work from. When she is five or six, the child will have a Dutch Colonial dollhouse that looks like the one her father grew up in.

Tom also asks his clients to supply a Bible verse for the underside of the house. We saw it not too long ago, furrowed into the wood in Adam's own hand, like a lover's initials carved on a tree:

"Peace be to this house."
—*Luke* 10:5
Love, Daddy

With the dollhouse, as with the other birthday gifts, he is putting his shoulder hard against the door separating time from eternity. He himself already has one foot in eternity, but this child will be a creature of her own generation. She will know and say things we can't imagine, and face challenges we don't want to imagine. It will be years before she becomes fascinated with him and pounds her fists against the same locked door.

Love, Daddy. With that, the door gives a little, almost cracks. You can feel the elemental power of love testing its own limits. He *was* able to love his unborn daughter and not merely an idea of her, just as we are still capable of loving *him* and not just a memory of him.

The eighteen gifts and the dollhouse occupy the same borderland as the birthing classes he and Jenny attend. With the Lamaze classes he is forging another material connection between himself and the future. "I'll be her coach," he tells Sarah confidently. "I have to help Jenny breathe," he says, alluding to the controlled breathing techniques she is learning.

The future is the baby waiting to be born.

As the month of June wears on and his strength begins to fail, he worries about his stamina holding up during a long labor. He speaks more frequently of "being there" for the delivery but in a secondary role to a professional delivery coach. He asks us if we would be willing to pick them up and drive them to the hospital when the day comes, since he won't be driving. Finally, he telephones his sister, asking her to coach Jenny through labor. This birth will still be a "miracle," he insists, but his role in it is diminishing. That door is closing too.

With our purchase in the bag, we head to a mall café for our refreshments. It is adorned with beach umbrellas and bathed in the music of the Caribbean. In the jewelry store I sensed that his hesitation over the more expensive bracelet had something to do with its price, and so I return to the subject. "You aren't made of money, you know. Why don't you at least let me help."

At the mention of financial dealing, his mental file server selects one of the many set pieces he has memorized over the years, this one from one of his favorite films, *Good Will Hunting*. We are sitting in our beachfront café, drinking coffee (or at least I am), and he is riffing into my ear Ben Affleck's blue-collar Chuckie: "Allegedly, your situation for you would be concurrently improved if I had two hundred dollars in my back pocket right now. . . . Until that day comes, keep your ear to the grindstone."

I do love this horsing around with him. "See, as long as we can hang out at the mall and you can make me laugh, I refuse to wear sackcloth and ashes," I say a little too enthusiastically. "We're walking around heah" (doing a little Chuckie myself). He is somewhat alarmed by my enthusiasm and replies with his palms on the table, "Okay," but in a tone that says, "Relax."

We are in such a good, loose mood that we casually break

another rule, this one against reminiscing. To talk about the past these days seems dangerously close to summing up a life. But with the bracelet in the bag, our snacks going nicely, and the entire future off limits, we have nowhere to go but the past.

My son and I have what G. K. Chesterton called "the slow maturing of old jokes," and today they appear to be approaching their maturation date. The set pieces are so familiar to us we can identify them by their code names: Paper Route, Cardinals in Atlanta, A Day on the *Kennedy*, Roommate on Drugs, Bar Exam Hell, Lost on the River, and quite a few others.

"Well, at least we had our Paper Route," I open, identifying the piece we are about to perform. "When I was a kid I had to go out every day at five in the morning . . ."

"But on Sundays the *Globe-Democrat* was too heavy, so PaPa drove you in the Gray Ghost," he says, completing my sentence. He even knows the name of the defunct St. Louis newspaper and the nickname for our family's 1953 Dodge. This is a prelude to the story of *his* paper route, which was really *our* paper route because we did it together. The *Advertisers* were dumped by the hundreds on our front porch every Tuesday to be banded for delivery on Wednesday at the latest. He didn't like the banding part and sometimes let the papers pile up in the living room for a few days, filling the house with the odor of damp newsprint and petroleum. He didn't like the delivery part either, because by the time we loaded the bag it was too heavy for him to carry on his bike.

Our solution was that we would pile the papers in the back

of our station wagon and I would troll through the neighborhood, with him perched dangerously on the tailgate of the
wagon tossing out the papers. Many of his tosses landed on the
roofs of houses or in the bushes.

This paper route was fun.

"But you always had something to do on Wednesday
nights," he remembers.

"And you never got the papers banded till Friday," I counter. "And when we were finished, you always had twenty left-
overs. What exactly did you do with them?" I ask, although
there was never a time when I didn't know.

As winter came on, we decided that the weather was too
cold to deliver the papers at night with the tailgate open to
the elements. That decision took us to Saturday afternoons,
which was usually reserved for college football.

We hated our paper route.

In the end, the distributor wrote Adam a letter of termina-
tion, which I delivered to him in Duke Medical Center, where
he was spending the night with a case of pneumonia. With
the crest of the *Advertiser* on the letterhead, it was the most
official document he had ever received. He was both honored
and bemused: although the pink slip was addressed to him,
Mr. Richard Adam Lischer, he knew we had both been let go.

We received the letter on his fourteenth birthday, January 28, 1986. The rest of the world remembers it as the day
the *Challenger* exploded like a Roman candle in the winter
sky. On this afternoon in the mall we are remembering it for
the umpteenth and last time as the day we got fired from our
paper route.

. . .

Sometimes I say to Tracy, "You know what I regret? I regret that I never took Adam camping. Or fly-fishing in Montana. I wish we had done some serious climbing in the Rockies. Damn."

Tracy replies, "Which mountain in the Rockies did you have in mind?"

Whenever I mentioned my regret to my grown son, he would reply indignantly, "What do you *mean* no adventure? We'll always have the Eno."

He says it again today in our Caribbean café. "You should have tied a bandana on one of the trees on the bank," he opens. "Maybe we wouldn't have gotten lost on the river."

"It was a good day for the Underwear Brothers," I reply. He has a good laugh at the thought of the two of us swimming in the Eno River in our underwear.

"The trouble was," he remembers, "you had just hurt your back. And we were always pulling the canoe over the rocks."

"Trouble was, it got late, we got lost and missed our port."

We beached the boat and pulled it over some rocks about a third of the way up a steep embankment. Then Adam and I shinnied through the mud the rest of the way up. We made our way to an unfamiliar asphalt road and simply stood there dirty and exhausted. The only mark of civilization was a small sign advertising a Primitive Baptist church.

We have come to the plateau of the first punch line. He will never forget that I stood in the road and hitchhiked while he hid in the weeds. "You said to me, 'We are going to do that thing I have always said if I catch you doing it I will beat your butt.'"

"You mean we're going to *hitchhike*?" I say, trying my best to imitate a boy of ten.

We have now approached the second punch line. A few decent, Baptist cars passed until, finally, two guys in a filthy Grand Am pulled over and offered us a ride. One of them wore a Hawaiian shirt, the other had no shirt. "Hop in, pohdners," says the guy in the shirt. They were smoking weed, and the back of the car was littered with beer cans.

Adam loves this part. One of the guys turns and leans across the seat toward us, friendly-like. "Beer?" he says.

I say, "You looked at me as if splitting a cold one was a genuine option." At that, Adam tips his chair back and laughs toward the ceiling. We are really into it now. With every telling, the soup thickens: in this version we are a little more desperately lost than before, a bit muddier as we shinny up the embankment, our rescuers slightly more stoned than in earlier accounts.

But, too quickly, we've come to the last line in the story. It's the third and final punch line. The two men in the Grand Am drop us at a convenience store where we can make a phone call to Tracy. As they weave their way down the road, they perform their roles to perfection, and one of them calls back to Adam and me, "Give peace a chance." Even my ten-year-old knows this is a somewhat dated phrase.

"Give peace a chance," we say in unison in the Caribbean café.

The end.

The key to the story is remembering the same points,

reciting them together, and laughing at the same punch lines, which we are doing as rehearsed. We have always done it this way—until now.

Today I have taken a wrong turn and gotten lost on another part of the river. Mentally, I'm still back in the cove where the Eno runs unusually deep and not a sound can be heard from other boaters or the tumble of modest water-falls downstream. Beneath a canopy of river birch, willow, and summer sky the two of us are laughing and spurting brown water through our teeth and diving for my baseball cap. We swim in circles round and round one another in a pool of mottled light, as if each were the other's shore. We have forgotten about the drifting boat and the lateness of the hour.

The waitress at the café pops in at our table, as if to create an intermission between our stories. We accept a second pot of tea and another cup of coffee, some nutty cake that he can't eat, and move into new territory.

He tells me that now, in his present stage of spiritual development, he regrets that he wasn't more faithful as a teenager. I tell him that adolescence is not famous for its spiritual depth. We agree that most teenage boys care about girls and sports, usually in that order. "Now I'm down to one girl," he says, "and am I glad of that. No, two!" he adds with something close to glee.

"Do you go to confession?" I asked. It is an honest question posed by someone who has never been.

"Sure," he says, "but I haven't been a Catholic long enough to have much to confess."

"What? Your Protestant sins don't count?" I ask as half question, half joke.

"I'll be damned if I'm going back to that high school junk," he says.

"If we started confessing all the boring stuff fathers and sons do to each other, where would it end? Think of all the mistakes I made raising you," I say. "And, trust me, I haven't forgotten them. Oh, God, think of my temper, Adam, just think of it! And all the rest of it." We both pause and let our minds wander back to the rest of it.

I remember the day he came home with a terrific role in his high school's production of *Anything Goes*. He was bursting with pleasure: "You won't believe what happened today! I got Moonface Martin!" Without so much as a word of congratulations, I promptly asked him if the play would interfere with his studies. I can still see his face falling. That was not a fight, but worse than a fight.

The parent's greatest failures, however, are the systemic omissions that occur over a lifetime and can be summed up with the phrase "failure to protect." We put you under the grace of God and convinced ourselves that your life was charmed, blessed, and secure. "Son, when you talked about monsters, your mother and I should have told you some of them are real. We lied. Evenings when you go to sleep, fourteen angels their watch do *not* keep. You are not protected. Sometimes your guardian angels turn out to be crows and vultures."

"You didn't have other sons to practice on," he answers, interrupting my deepening vacancy. "I never give your mistakes a thought."

"I've been relying on your forgiveness for years."

"You can do that," he says, and smiles shyly.

We are absolving one another of having occupied the same time and space—of having lived under the same roof, cluttered the same bathroom, scrounged the same French fries, dipped into the same hormone pool, adored and bedeviled the same two women, and shared the same unstable temperament—all at close quarters and in the most god-awful phases of our lives: his adolescence and my middle age.

Wipe it clean! Wipe it clean! But love it all. That's the way we are feeling in our mall café.

The time is coming, in a month or less, when I will simply kiss his unresisting head and say Thank you for everything, thank you, thank you, thank you, and he will look up intently at me and absorb my love without changing expression. But today we are talking up a storm.

The server has returned. Perhaps she has noticed that we are using this site as a church when it was designed to be a shrine on the way to Williams-Sonoma. Her manner lets us know these tables can't be tied up indefinitely. We've done two pots of tea, multiple coffees, and some cake. This is not a destination. "Anything more I can get you guys? Or will that be it?" In other words, it might be time for you two to move on.

. . .

It is still June, and my Father's Day card arrives several days early, as if the sender has found the perfect sentiment and can't wait to convey it. Obviously designed for a stepfather or a favorite uncle, it reads, "You've been like a father to me." This has been going on for several years, ever since I inadvertently sent him a valentine on his birthday.

My Father's Day present this year will be an outing to a Durham Bulls baseball game. I gather from comments Jenny has made that Adam considers the ball game, like our recent trip to the mall, a gift to me, the gift of himself. I will later learn from Jenny that he has taken a staggering amount of OxyContin to make it through the evening.

Adam likes baseball but has not completely surrendered himself to the game. He has not memorized the starting lineup of the 1968 St. Louis Cardinals as I have, doesn't go weak in the knees at the mention of Stan Musial as I do, and never had a mother who once sold his baseball cards, as I did. I got him started playing Little League when he was too young and still afraid of the pitched ball, when he was thrilled to be assigned to play right field but couldn't *find* right field. In those days, he ran the bases like a firefly at dusk, skipping second or third base when he felt like it, totally innocent of the immutable laws by which baseball is governed.

Adam is a socially intelligent baseball fan, able to maintain an acceptable level of patter with little effort. He is apt to inject phrases like "good field, no hit" or "high hard one" into any conversation, but he does not understand the finer points of the game, like the infield fly rule or the double switch. Whenever he doesn't know what to say, he reverts to Tracy's all-purpose sports comment that works in every conceivable situation: "I'm not surprised."

He knows I understand the Mysteries, and God knows I am an all-too-willing instructor. We have been through this before. I tell him the Durham shortstop will never make it in the big leagues because he can't field. Later, when he makes his third error of the game, Adam looks at me solemnly and says, "There you go." Because it is Father's Day, he treats my knowledge of baseball trivia with genuine respect, as if this information is impressive and will come in handy some day.

This night will be our final outing as father and son, the very last time we will commune through the shared acoustics of a minor-league baseball game, amidst the *no-batter*s and *hum-babe*s of a summer evening. It is the last time I will educate him, and it is the last time he will say, "There you go."

It is the sort of June night that requires only a baseball game to complete its perfection. We arrive early enough to watch both teams take batting practice. He has bought good seats, perhaps too good, since they are located just behind the visiting team's dugout, which means we will be targets for foul balls and screaming line drives off the bats of right-handed hitters. When he was a kid we would have constructed a game of being afraid. He mentions it first thing. "We could get brained in these seats."

Baseball, especially as the Durham Bulls play it, provides an undemanding background for leisurely conversation, like a jazz guitar at a cocktail party, and that is how Adam and I are using the game. Yet we are keeping a wary eye on every ball that jumps off the bat.

At the seventh-inning stretch, we stand to sing "Take Me

Out to the Ball Game," and Adam says, "I propose a toast: Father's Day, next year, right here at the old ballpark." He says it with very little conviction, and I nod, weakly. We clink our plastic cups of Coke and beer, and return our attention to the game.

It is clear that Adam means this to be a full outing and not a symbolic exercise. We leave in the top of the ninth so we have time to get something to eat. We walk across the street to an outdoor café in the newly refurbished American Tobacco Campus. Since our last outing at the mall, his pace has slowed by half. We enter at the back of the restaurant and move at a snail's pace past all the tables and the ballgame crowd to the hostess station. "Just one?" the young woman asks. "No, two," he says as if making a point. She takes a good look at Adam and waves him quickly to the nearest table.

While we wait for our food, he tells me what a wonderful wife he has, as if Jenny were a stranger to me, and repeats everything he has already told me about their evening ritual of candle-lighting, reading, and prayer. Once again, he goes over their morning routine, the anointing with sacred water, the restorative cup of tea. He recites the last half of the Shakespearean sonnet that hangs in their foyer, the one that promises,

> Love alters not with his brief hours and weeks,
> But bears it out even to the edge of doom.

We are running out of things to say.

Then, as if introducing a subject that needs no introduction, he says, "I wonder what it's like to die." The question itself is an act of love. He understands how incapacitated I am by his impending death, and he wants to help me say good-bye, or if not to say it, to help me approach the outskirts of saying it. It is his way of letting me know that I am worthy of such a conversation, and it's his method of protecting me from future regret or self-recrimination. *See,* he is implying with this offer, *there isn't anything we were afraid to talk about; we covered our bases.*

"I've thought so much about what comes after death that I haven't considered death itself. I think Jesus is waiting for you," I say, barely suppressing my emotion. "You join a great communion of souls. You . . ."

"Not *after* death, but dying," he clarifies. "The act, the event."

"I don't know. I wish I knew. I don't think of it as an event."

We both want dying to be a procession of dots that gradually fades until they disappear. We do not want it to be the tangent that grazes the crystal sphere and, touching it, shatters it. Together, we treat the subject with the realism and the mystery it deserves. Adam and I decide that the act of dying is more like manual labor to be done in this life. It is a work and, as such, the mystery of it is overrated. We move off the subject not because we are made uncomfortable by it, but because we have done our duty and can't come up with a better answer.

Finally, he answers his own question. "It's walking through the door into another room."

"You won't be alone," I say.

"Right," he says, with a finality that ends the conversation. "It's overrated."

Then we fall back into our old routine of hanging out, and with that a comfortable patch of stillness settles over us. Our words to one another were never original or profound, but now we don't need them at all, not to clarify anything between us, not to speculate on the mystery of death, not even to break a longish silence. We have been here before, but this time it feels like a place to which we will not return.

When we get to his house I walk him from the car across the pea gravel to his front door, as if we're a couple of teen-agers tentatively completing a first date.

"Well thanks," I say, "I had a lovely Father's Day."

"Yeah, man, let's do it again."

Cross

13

On the Wednesday after our Father's Day's outing, while he and Jenny were saying their prayers before the altar at Immaculate Conception, Adam had a massive seizure. They had walked from the small chapel through the gathering space into the main sanctuary as they often did after Mass, where they would pray for themselves and the baby, and offer intercessions for others. They were alone in the enormous church when he fell. Jenny ran to get help and then returned and waited with him until the medics arrived. He was taken by ambulance from the church to Duke Medical Center.

I found him in the ER. He was framed in a large observation window in a room adjacent to the nurses' station. The room was brutally white to the last detail and ablaze with fluorescent light. Jenny and Tracy were positioned on each side of him at the head of his bed. He was not speaking and his eyes were closed. Wrapped and bound in a coarse white sheet, he looked like a corpse prepared for burial.

Jenny sat quietly, and Tracy patted him as she told me what little there was to tell. The seizure was caused by the swelling in his brain. He had been given the steroid Decadron to reduce the swelling and Dilantin to control the seizure activity. He moved in and out of sleep. Father Steve came from the church to pray. Appearing at the foot of Adam's bed in his brown cloak and cowl, it was as if he had entered the family sepulcher.

While we sat with him in the observation room Adam had a second, powerful seizure. He suddenly lost consciousness, and his body began to struggle violently like that of a prisoner under restraints. Tracy sat by his head and tried to comfort him while nurses and the ER doctor attended to him. One of them injected him with Ativan to stop the convulsions.

I tried to usher Jenny away from the scene, but we stalled in the doorway as we watched the seizure run its course. It was the second time she had witnessed his shattering; it was my first, and what was happening to him under these burning lights was almost more than I could bear.

When he came out of it, he looked up at her and said with a depth of feeling, "I'm sorry, baby." He said it as if he knew exactly where he'd been and what it must have cost her to watch.

She said, "I'm sorry too."

Once he was fully conscious and stabilized, Adam was admitted to a room in the hospital. Jenny later told me that she thought this might be the end, but soon he was eating and talking again, even as the massive doses of steroids used to control the swelling in his brain produced painfully slow, dystonic movements in his hands and arms. He did not seem to notice, or at least he didn't mention them, and after the first night they disappeared.

He quickly made friends with the nurses and staff on the floor. Hospitalization brought a new company of medical helpers and chaplains into his life. His oncologist and other caregivers disappeared and were replaced by continuous shifts of friendly, competent strangers who took his blood, weighed him, bathed him, fed him, and checked his Dilantin levels.

Once his condition began to stabilize, Adam seemed to enjoy his new surroundings. He had arrived at the ER "confabulating," as his medical record puts it, filling in the blank spots of his memory with stories he believed to be true. He claimed that he and the EMTs had stopped on the way to the hospital for coffee and a ham sandwich. He had a new audience for his confabulations, and Tracy, Jenny, and I had a little time off.

Throughout his stay Adam was cheerful and funny as ever. When a resident suggested suppositories for the emergency treatment of convulsions, Adam expressed some reservations (as did we all). Then he deadpanned, "What little dignity I have left, I cling to."

One afternoon I walked him and his IV pole into the bathroom, where we had a brief Laurel and Hardy moment. We fumbled him out of two hospital gowns, one tied in the front, the other in the back, without losing the IV lines in the process. With him buck naked, we managed to drop one of the gowns in the toilet and partially flush it down. "Oh, well done," I said. "Oh, well done yourself," he replied. Later I heard him say to Jenny, "Now that he takes me to the bathroom, he thinks he controls my bladder too."

On his second day in the hospital, my colleague Teresa Berger visited him in his room. She came as a new friend of Adam's and also in her capacity as a Eucharistic minister at Immaculate Conception. She brought the consecrated Host from Mass and served it to Adam and Jenny from the adjustable hospital tray across his bed. "Adam," she said, "the Body of Christ for you."

Afterward, as I watched Adam chatting and laughing with her, it occurred to me that he was suddenly *on* for a new and appreciative audience of one. He seemed completely at ease with her; she appeared charmed by his smile.

He said, "Teresa, you know I had my seizure while I was in the church asking God for healing. [*Pause, beat.*] He sure got back to me in a hurry."

Not giving in to the joke, Teresa asked him what he wanted most from God. "What is your heart's desire?"

He answered, "Healing," but quickly undercut his reply by asking for one of his dogs to stay with him. Then he gave her his best smile.

Not giving in to the smile, Teresa persisted, "Tell me your second choice, Adam. If you can't have your heart's desire, what's next on your list?"

He immediately recognized the pastoral nature of her question, and his demeanor changed. Gone was the big smile and the rapid-fire comeback. No wink for the witness or honest tear for the jury. "Why don't you give me a few days to think it over," he said, and made no further reply.

. . .

When the children were small, Tracy organized a family fire drill. In case of fire, she said, we would gather at a large tree stump at the bottom of the front yard. That way we'd know if one of us was missing or needed rescuing. I thought of our fire drill every time Tracy, Sarah, and I met late in the evening in the hospital cafeteria. In the quiet hours, the cafeteria had become our place of refuge. The three of us would sit in the half-lit coffee bar and talk about the Missing One and try to come to terms with what was happening to him and our family.

Late one afternoon Tracy and I were joined in the cafeteria by an old friend of Adam's named Don, who once had been his training master in Tae Kwon Do during Adam's college days in Chapel Hill. When he heard of Adam's illness, he respectfully asked permission to reenter his life as if he were about to enter a restricted area. It was immediately clear to us that Don cared deeply for Adam but also had an agenda, one that Adam would come to understand and fully accept.

As we sat and talked with Don in the cafeteria, Tracy and I began to understand the deeper thing that was at work between Don and our son.

We thought it was unusual how animated he became when he talked about his late father, a successful developer on the West Coast. "He was the sort of man who when he entered a room he took it over," he said. "He had the one thing I will never be able to duplicate: charisma." Then, with his intense blue eyes studying our faces, he explained himself. "My father died of cancer just after I was born. I live in the shadow of a man I never knew." What he clearly wanted to know first-hand was the emotional disposition of a dying father toward his unborn child. For that he needed Adam.

But Adam also needed him. Don told us how he had discovered an old tape recording of his father's voice and how much it continued to mean to him. The message on the tape was not addressed to him, but he listened to it as if his father were speaking directly to him. It was clear to us that Don was gently urging Adam to make a film or tape for his daughter.

Suddenly, we could see two lessons in progress: the older man was tutoring Adam in the longings of a child who has never met her daddy. She will want to hear his voice, see lots of photos, perhaps a film clip or two. She will need some little sacrament of him without being overpowered by his charisma. But Adam was rapidly losing ground to his disease. Things were moving too fast. He was reluctant to be preserved in high-resolution technology that would leave no play to the child's imagination.

At the same time, Adam was teaching Don an important lesson. Adam could imagine that his own little girl would one day ask about his love for her. She would wonder what he thought of her and what he hoped for her. Had he any real sense of her at all?

The older man was still haunted by these questions and had turned to Adam as to an oracle. In traditional cultures, the terminally ill person is treated as a source of sacred wisdom, and Adam was willing to accept a version of this role. What he gave his friend over the next few weeks was a pastorally guided tour through the heart of a young father who is about to say good-bye to his baby. He explained to him in what sense he knew and loved his daughter, and, like a trainer or a tutor, he demonstrated just how extravagantly a dying man can love a child he has never met.

The hospital cafeteria contained the suffering and emotional overflow from hundreds of rooms. It was also the noisiest and most unreflective space in the entire building. In the midst of the clatter it was not uncommon to see people sitting in place weeping over their trays or simply staring into space. Some stood like statues on the terrace just outside the large windows or like exiles in the smokers' court in the distance.

I was eating off my tray at a long, closely spaced line of tables near the center of the room, when out of the undercurrent of noise, I slowly began to absorb a conversation in progress not three feet from me. From the next table a single sentence broke through: "I've got to go to Charlotte this weekend for a baby shower." It was spoken by a middle-aged woman to a younger blond woman. The sentence caught my attention because I knew Jenny's aunt was giving a baby shower in Charlotte on Sunday. Jenny and Adam, of course, would not be able to attend.

Amidst the many sounds in the cafeteria, this conversation was all I could hear. The older of the two continued, "It's for the daughter of my best friend. She's originally from Charlotte. Her husband is dying of cancer. And her with a baby due in a month."

The younger woman said with an absence of exclamation, "What a story."

"Yes, it's so sad."

This narrative had to stop. I could not contain myself. I leaned across the table and rudely interrupted their conversation: "It's my son." I might as well have vomited onto their chicken salad. They looked at me as if I were a crazy man.

"It's my son," I clarified. "That you're talking about. *Who* you're talking about. His name is Adam. I'm the father, Richard. Jenny is my daughter-in-law. They're here now. Upstairs."

They quickly grasped what I was saying, and the three of us regained our composure. It was not an embarrassing moment for them or an angry incident for me because they had not said anything objectionable. One woman had given a factual report, and her companion had responded dispassionately to the plight of two people she didn't know.

It was the word "story" that later triggered something in me. I remembered one of Sarah's comments a few days after Adam's recurrence of cancer. "I never dreamed this would be our family's story."

We have become the characters in other people's narratives, I thought, *and it is* so sad.

No matter how complicated the story, there are only two plots you can feel in your gut: stories of the fortunate and stories of the unfortunate, and only the thinnest of lines separates one from the other. The winners live above the line, the losers live below it.

For most of our lives our family had managed to stay on the upside of that line. We flirted with the downside when Adam was struggling with his neurological disorder, when other kids made fun of him and adults pitied him, but by the grace of God we had shinnied over that one and were living in positive territory. On the downside of the line are the poor, people with AIDS, victims of random violence, the uneducated, the unemployed, the unloved, the unlovable, the hopelessly depressed, and those who die young.

The young woman's use of "story" confirmed that we had slipped into a pool of misfortune so fathomless that the line was no longer visible above us. The water in the lagoon was still clear but alarmingly deep. Among our acquaintances, the shorthand notation "Lischer" now calls up "loss," and no matter what good fortune may come our way, nobody wants our life. They often begin their condolences with the sentence, "I can't imagine . . ."

But of course they can. We all can. That's why we tell stories.

"Things are so bad in Zimbabwe," an acquaintance of mine said recently, "that the average life expectancy for a male is 34.4 years. Can you imagine that?" He must have noticed something in my eyes because he paused and then added apologetically, "He was younger than that, wasn't he?"

There are only a few plots in the world, but every one of them hinges on death. Death is the ultimate sanction. It lends its edge to every tale, whether an action-adventure film or *Romeo and Juliet*. Everything in the story either anticipates death or responds to it. *Pay attention,* the author or screenwriter warns, *somebody might die.* The only mystery is: by what contrivance of plot will it happen or be avoided?

Two weeks before Adam's re-diagnosis, I participated in the stripping of the altar at a Maundy Thursday worship service. It is one of the many ways the church has of dramatizing the story of Jesus. On Maundy Thursday the story is not one of conflict with evil, but of one man's inexorable reduction from the status of God to that of mortal. His friends desert him. He loses his self-control in the Garden of Gethsemane. The last shreds of his dignity are taken from him in a ritual of public shaming and execution. Finally, even his Father abandons him.

At the end of the service, members of the congregation remove all decorations, books, and symbols from the chancel. One of them even lifts the purple stole from the minister's shoulders. Finally, two women strip the altar of the fair linen at the top, then the horizontal band across the front, and finally the larger and more ornate frontal, until all that is left is raw wood.

Undressing an altar, like undressing a person, or a body, is a work of exquisite care. When everything is removed what is left is nude and vulnerable. Not as imposing as we expected. It seems almost a shame to see the altar that way, and so when the women are finished undressing it someone turns out the lights and the congregation files out in silence.

A beautiful vessel brimming with love is being stripped to its most elemental quality. Every day something is taken away from him. He is not being robbed like the children of Africa, but he is being purified. Soon only his soul will be visible.

What a story.

In late June, after Adam returned home from the hospital, I began visiting cemeteries in our area. It was time. I had helped him find an apartment in Washington, and Tracy and I had done the same in Raleigh after law school. This bit of reconnoitering was merely a continuation of what we had always done.

But this time I did it in secret. How could I support Adam's decision to continue with chemotherapy and at the same time look for a place to bury him? Visiting cemeteries was not something Team Adam could do as a group because, as those who had pledged to support him in his fight against cancer, we would have been undermining our solidarity with him and his trust in us. Jenny and Adam were maintaining a faithful openness to the future. How could I tell them I was grave shopping?

One afternoon I rode in a little motorized cart among the 22,000 graves in Durham's Maplewood Cemetery. My guide was the director of field operations, a helpful man who informed me that the older, picturesque sections of the cemetery were long closed. Along the way I received an education in the qualities one looks for in a final resting place. We spoke of view and elevation: from exclusive sections of the cemetery one can "see" the tower of Duke Chapel in the distance; one should also consider drainage and avoid the low spots where rain water pools. We even discussed the neighbors—not the neighborhood bordering the cemetery, but the relative fame or infamy of those who might be buried nearby.

A friend of mine suggested I look at St. Mary's in Orange County. The cemetery was created in 1759, but on the registry of Orange County cemeteries it is listed as "disused." A small and unkempt clearing in a densely wooded area, it is virtually inaccessible from either the church or the road.

I then visited St. Matthew's Catholic Cemetery in north

Durham County near the Orange County line. Its graceful hills lie beside a small, new church in the green farmland of the Piedmont. The church's bells ring at the close of day. I made a mental note of St. Matthew's against that day when time would be short and decisions would come with only the greatest difficulty.

Adam said little about his final resting place. He wanted a location that would be safe for Jenny and the baby to visit, as though a cemetery were just another neighborhood where he would live and where we would want to spend some time with him. His new place in the country would become a kind of second home to us all, we thought. It would be nice if there were some trees nearby, a bench, and a church to pray in. We wanted a mowed and stately place, a small city of the dead like the cemetery in *Our Town,* where the residents chat among themselves and on special occasions interact with the living. We wanted a simple extension of our world into his.

Then, in late June or early July, Adam asked his mother if he could be buried in the meadow in front of our house.

Several years earlier we had left our old neighborhood and bought a house in the rural buffer of Orange County between Durham and Chapel Hill. By the time we got the place the meadow was slowly being taken over by pine and cedar volunteers. We had most of them bush-hogged and began mowing it in late spring after the wildflowers finished blooming. The meadow is neatly dotted with individual cedar trees, including one the grandchildren call the Climbing Tree, and one modest grove with two tall pines, a cedar, a poplar, and a candelabra-shaped maple. A small concrete figure of an angel already rests beneath the maple. I suspect Adam had the grove in mind for himself.

When Tracy told me of his request, I was glad to hear it. The meadow had always been my first choice, but I had never said so.

We quickly contacted a landscape architect with extensive experience in burial grounds, and he came out one Saturday morning and walked the property with Tracy and me and his dog. We spent a couple of hours exploring some lovely sites for a family cemetery in the meadow, well away from the Climbing Tree.

When I called the county Department of Environmental Health, I learned that cemeteries are one of the last bastions of deregulation. All that is required is a visit from the environmental engineer; no permit is needed, and the Health Department plays no role.

There are 285 cemeteries in Orange County, most of them family burial grounds. The more I studied the Registry of Cemeteries and read the field descriptions, however, the more I began to doubt the wisdom of creating Cemetery #286. Our land will not likely be occupied by the next generation of our family. One day our acreage may be home to the houses of strangers with poured driveways, installed gas grills, and a nearby Stop N Go.

The Registry locates the fragments of one family burial ground "under three large hackberry trees . . . marked by some wooden posts." Of another—a "black and white" graveyard—it says, "Cemetery is barely visible on rocky terrain now used as a trash dump."

Despite these caution signs, I continued to favor Adam's idea. We aren't the administrators of the future, I said to Tracy. All that is required for a burial is some dirt and some hope in God's promise.

For me, Adam's request closed the circle that had begun with our first parish in southern Illinois and the graveyard behind the parsonage. It was there we learned to be comfortable living among dead people we had never known. If we granted his request, we would not make occasional visits to his world; he would take up permanent residence in ours.

Adam had approached his mother first, probably because he knew that hers would be the toughest vote. Tracy had reacted to his request with something close to revulsion. Nor did she think much of my romanticized view of cemeteries. Nevertheless, because Adam had made the request, she promised him she would talk to me, even as she gently explained to him how it would pierce her heart to have his grave in daily view.

"These aren't the graves of strangers from the last generation," she said to me in private. "This is our son. Can you imagine driving up that long gravel road every day with Adam's marker in the grove?"

We turned to Sarah for advice; Sarah agreed with her mother. She helped me see the emotional folly of living with the beloved dead.

After we had made our decision, I pulled down my volume of Robert Frost and reread "Home Burial." The poem tells how a married couple is divided by the presence of their child's "mound" on their property. The wife is inconsolable, always "Looking back over her shoulder at some fear," while her husband is capable of complaining about the weather, rotting fences, and other mundane matters. Her grief is raw and resentful; his is real, too, but it has produced an unfeeling hardness in him. The boy's grave has come between them.

I called the landscaper and the Orange County people and quickly put a stop to our family cemetery.

Tracy told Adam of our decision, which he appeared to accept and understand completely. Later, when we approached him about a "nice Catholic cemetery in the country," he had no interest in visiting it, and he never again spoke of his final resting place.

14

July in the North Carolina Piedmont is not the best month for dying or giving birth. Wrestling with life at either of its extremities is made sweaty and oppressive by the heat. Just catching your breath can be pure aggravation, as it was for Adam and his very pregnant Jenny, both of whom were moving ever more deliberately through their summer days. If you complain to a Durham native about the heat, he might respond, "Not as hot as Fayetteville," but that's about as much relief as you'll get.

We slipped through the vapors from one air-conditioned refuge to another: from the lower level of Adam and Jenny's house, to the grotto-like sanctuary of Immaculate Conception, to the frigid hospital for bone marrow boosters.

We went about our business as if his hospitalization had cured him of the swelling in his brain and he was free to resume his normal activities. But the heat aggravated his nausea and pain, and the Zofran made him shiver with cold. Adam and Jenny made it to Mass every morning, but now he was having occasional half seizures and brief moments of unconsciousness, sometimes called "absence seizures." When he was in the hospital we had read from Psalm 50, "Call upon me in the day of trouble; / I will deliver you." That day was bearing down on us.

He had one of these "absences" on the way to our house on the Fourth of July and arrived ashen-faced and shaken. He rested for a moment on the banquette in the breakfast room, but the glare from the skylights was too much for him. Cane in hand, he slowly moved to the shaded area with lower ceilings at the back of the house. He set his cane to one side and formally arranged himself like an older gentleman on the low-slung sectional in the family room, where he held court for family members and friends.

Jenny followed a half step behind him, as if to shelter him, her body moving in perfect harmony with his. Eight and a half months pregnant, she was doing nothing for herself and everything for him. She brought him something to drink, reminded him of his medication, stooped to retrieve his cane, but most of all she followed him with her eyes.

This is how life is held together, I thought. You gather your family, play cards, and put on some music while Dad stands over the grill and sweats in the midday heat. As the meat begins to brown he shouts, "Five minutes! Five minutes!" through double-glazed glass at air-conditioned people who cannot hear him.

If you observe the Fourth and keep the feast exactly as it has always been done, if you have a baseball game on TV with the sound turned down, if you set the table as you always have and everyone sits in their usual places—if you reproduce the simple contentments of a lifetime—he will not die. This is how life is held together.

Adam played a game of Crazy Eights with his nephew Luke while he held six-month-old Calvin on his lap. He allowed Tracy to put her arms around him and give him extra hugs and kisses. And yet the more snugly the family drew around him the more elusively he moved among us. He was drifting away like a boat cut free of its moorings.

Teresa came to say good-bye before leaving for her home in Germany. It was then in our family room, seven days after he had been released from the hospital, that she renewed her question, "Next to healing, what do you want?" and he gave her his answer.

"I want peace," he said. "And I want it for Jenny and . . . " With the movement of his hand, he included the baby.

The next day, on the fifth, I picked up Adam and took him to the back door of Oncology where he slipped in for his G-CSF, a plasma booster shot. The nurse called it "Miracle Grow."

From there we drove to a nearby Barnes & Noble for a talk and book signing by his childhood basketball idol Gene Banks.

We had a lot to remember and laugh about on July 5, even though by this time Adam's body was loaded with every imaginable drug: OxyContin for pain, Zoloft for anxiety, Paxil for depression, Zofran for nausea, Benadryl to sleep, Protonix for reflux, Peri-Colace for constipation, Decadron for swelling, and Dilantin for seizures. That he was able to walk across the parking lot, much less smile at the thought of meeting the great Gene Banks, was a miracle.

When we got to the store, the event had been canceled.

We returned to his house and holed up in the cool lower level. The lights were off and the blinds were drawn. We played Celtics versus Lakers on PlayStation. It was as sad and pointless a morning as we ever passed together.

On Thursday I met my friend Maurice Ritchie for breakfast at the Mad Hatter. I could be comfortable with Maurice not only because he was an old friend, but because when Adam was diagnosed he had promised me, "I will go with you in this, as far as I am able."

It was about 9:15 and to our delight in walked Adam and Jenny after Mass. It is very hard to explain the joy I felt when I saw them. It was as if Adam had been away on a journey and I hadn't seen or touched him for years. They ate with us, and again I was seized by the conviction that anyone who can drink tea and tell stories cannot possibly die. I was so inspired by our meeting that I went home and wrote Adam a love letter, which I slipped into their mailbox later that afternoon. Until that day I had fully understood that he was a married man, soon to be a father, and no longer a child. He was my adult son and no longer my boy. With that letter I may have backslid a little.

By Friday of that week Team Adam was facing another treatment decision. Our consulting oncologist, the one who was holding a little something in reserve when all else failed, was advising Adam to begin another drug, Avastin. Adam's regular oncologist was guarded in his response because Avastin is associated with intracranial hemorrhage. True, the drug might enable Adam to live long enough to see the baby; or it might cause a hemorrhage and hasten his death. The two specialists were at loggerheads. Boundaries were being crossed and egos stepped upon, but that was for them to sort out, not us. Finally, despite his misgivings, the primary oncologist agreed to the new therapy.

In this, the eleventh hour, we received the only encouraging news of Adam's long ordeal. A last-minute CT scan ordered by his primary oncologist revealed that the largest of his brain tumors, the one in the frontal lobe, had not grown since the last scan. We took this as an indication that the latest therapy, a combination of Taxol and carboplatin, was having an effect. That was enough for everybody, including both doctors, to cancel the Avastin. Adam would not be subjected to a therapy that might hasten his death.

On Sunday we went to Mass with Adam and Jenny. Sarah had driven down from Charlottesville the day before, and she joined us at the service. At Immaculate Conception, with its nouveau Catholic casualness, its banners and minimalist paraments, its babbling children of every race and color, I could worship with an attentiveness I couldn't muster in my upstairs study at home. In this lively sanctuary I was never as terrifyingly alone with death—or God—as I was in the privacy of my own house.

As usual, the 9:30 Mass was filled with young married couples with babies and canvas bags stuffed with diapers, bottles, and other baby equipment. Everything was yielding pain that morning, even the routine evidence of other people's happiness. During Communion the congregation sang "On Eagle's Wings," which, as always, made Tracy and me cry.

And he will raise you up on eagle's wings,
Bear you on the breath of dawn,
Make you to shine like the sun,
And hold you in the palm of his hand.

The sermon was about suffering, and Father David confessed to his own inadequacy in the face of it.

For some time now the five of us had been attending to sermons in a new way. We listened for the word of God the way a dog on the back of a pickup truck flattens its ears and leans into the wind; we responded to the sermon's theme as if it were chosen with our family in mind (which it might have been). We absorbed the nuances of the spoken word, the imagery of each hymn, and the liturgy's every move, as if the entire package constituted a single promise to us.

We were worshiping as if our lives depended on it.

After Mass, Tracy and I brought in brunch from Foster's Market, and Sarah took photos of Adam and Jenny opening their presents from the baby shower in Charlotte. He is wearing the olive-colored linen shirt with long sleeves, open at the neck. We have examined the photos carefully, like forensic experts looking for clues; but all they reveal is a good-looking young man, early thirties if that old, surrounded by the remains of a lazy Sunday morning.

We left their house feeling that the day was covered. Church, brunch, the opening of gifts—the rest of the day we could imagine. Adam would take a short nap, they would walk the dog in Rockwood Park, share a pizza for supper, watch a movie, pray, and say good night and I love you to the baby.

We would all sleep well. We could continue a long time at this pace.

On Monday he and Jenny kept an ob-gyn appointment in Chapel Hill. That evening he called the whole family to his table, including his grandfather Bob. His only instructions were to bring Kentucky Fried Chicken "with plenty of sides." He was reverting to the good stuff. We prayed "Come Lord Jesus" and dived in.

As we were leaving he said to me with real enthusiasm, "I've just begun the best book." It was Bob Woodward's story of Deep Throat, *The Secret Man*.

On Tuesday morning Adam and Jenny went to Mass as usual. He rested in the day, and I went to the pharmacy to pick up more OxyContin. The pharmacist refused to fill the prescription because its dosage level was extraordinarily high. The doctor's PA confirmed the prescription by fax, and Tracy picked up the OxyContin late in the afternoon. Jenny invited her to stay for supper, which was peanut butter and jelly sandwiches made by Adam. He cleared off his own dishes.

Jenny noticed two things about Adam. He had become a quiet man. He was initiating fewer conversations, preferring, it seemed, to keep company with himself. And she noticed the peanut butter, a staple from his childhood. First Kentucky

Fried Chicken, now peanut butter sandwiches. *Adam is traveling back,* she thought.

That evening the men's basketball coach Mike Krzyzewski telephoned him to see how he was doing. Adam had once been a Duke ball boy, but Mike was calling in his capacity as a fellow parishioner at Immaculate Conception.

He invited Adam to the intervarsity scrimmage held every fall. Adam said, "Coach, I don't think you know what I'm up against." They talked about another basketball event, this one scheduled for later in the summer. Adam said he didn't think so, but he penciled it into his organizer.

A call from Coach K is a big deal, and before he went to bed that night he telephoned his sister to tell her all about it.

On Wednesday morning, July 13, three months to the day from Adam's re-diagnosis, the day when he called to say "Hey, *Dad,*" I awakened to a voice so unnaturally composed that I knew something terrible was happening.

Jenny said, "You might want to come over and be with Adam. He has an awful headache."

She had waited until exactly 6 a.m. before telephoning us.

On Tuesday evening he had experienced problems with depth perception for the first time. He had walked into a door. He was beginning to feel a buildup of pain in his head, but he had taken his medicine, hoped for the best, and gone to bed.

It came for him in earnest around five the next morning, and when it did there was no holding it back. He asked Jenny to read from the psalms to him, which she did by the light of a single lamp beside their bed. He closed his eyes and tried to absorb the ancient medicine directly through the outer membrane of his forehead and into his swollen brain.

> *Do not be far from me,*
> *for trouble is near*
> *and there is no one to help.*

> *You will not fear the terror of the night,*
> *nor the arrow that flies by day. . . .*
> *For he will give his angels charge of you*
> *to guard you in all your ways.*

The psalms did not make the pain stop, but they gave him peace from five o'clock until six that morning.

When we arrived, he was lying almost diagonally across the bed with his head and upper body supported by three or four pillows. The lights in the room were dim, but he kept his eyes steadfastly closed and squinted, shielding them with the crook of his arm, like a man who is dying under a desert sun. His shoulders and long body filled the double bed and made it look small. He was surrounded by his books, favorite things, and necessities: pill bottles, a psalter, prayer books, photographs, and Woodward's *The Secret Man* for bedtime reading. Clothes had been thrown off and on in a hurry; a duffel bag lay half packed. Adjoining their room, open to the living room below, lay a tiny nursery in perfect order.

It was 6:20 and Jenny was on the phone with the oncologist. With his eyes closed, Adam was whispering directions to her. "Tell him I need . . ."

She said, "It's never hurt like this before. His headache is unbearable."

"What?" he said impatiently when she got off the phone.

"You can have the OxyContin every hour." What she didn't say was that the doctor also advised her to call the hospice nurse.

The OxyContin did nothing.

Another call to the oncologist's PA, and Jenny returned with the message, "You can double it."

At 9:30 our pastor, Tom Colley, arrived for a prearranged appointment and climbed the winding stairs to Adam and Jenny's bedroom. Tom read the sentence from Psalm 31 that had come to summarize Adam's faith in this his final summer: "My times are in your hand."

The doubled OxyContin didn't work to relieve Adam's agony. With the hospice nurse on the way with a more powerful pain medication, Oncology decided that Adam should be admitted directly to a floor in the hospital. But there would be a delay because there were no rooms available. We waited.

In the crisis hour, when things couldn't get worse, they somehow did. When the hospice nurse was informed that we were trying to have Adam admitted to the hospital, she turned around and refused to come to the house. Jenny tried to explain—I could hear her pleading—that his hospitalization would have nothing to do with treatment, only the palliation of pain, but to no avail.

Tracy walked downstairs to the lower level and began compulsively ironing Adam's shirts.

A little before three o'clock, we were instructed to bring Adam to the ninth floor of Duke Medical Center. As we gathered his things and helped him up, he began vomiting, and we considered calling an ambulance, but he thought not. With Tracy and me supporting him on each side, he made it down the stairs and into our car. At the hospital we hailed a wheelchair and he was taken directly to the 9300 wing.

There were no rooms. Not on the ninth floor, not on *any* floor in the entire hospital.

He was admitted in a small visitors' alcove near one of the nurses' stations. There, while a nurse recorded the usual intake information, he was fitted to an IV and infused with Dilaudid. The nurses and his family, which now included Sarah, who had rushed down from Charlottesville to be with him, formed a tight little circle around his wheelchair while he received the fluids. Within one minute—*sixty seconds!*—he looked up at a nurse named Karen and sent her the sweetest smile imaginable, like a little boy who has just been given a popsicle on a hot summer's day. The pain was gone.

His left eyebrow now remained in an arched position, with his left eye half-closed. The resident asked him about it, but he professed not to have noticed. Whatever was occurring in his brain had left him with a permanently ironic expression, as if he had arrived at a settled attitude toward his own condition.

He was finally admitted to a room on Wednesday evening, more than twelve hours after the onset of his agony. Tracy and I visited with him into the evening while Jenny rushed home to collect necessities for an overnight stay at the hospital. We even watched some TV together until Jenny arrived at about nine o'clock.

As we drove home, it occurred to us both how little Adam had actually said that evening. "What exactly did he *say?*" we asked, but we came up with nothing. To most comments he offered only a word or two in reply along with his new crooked smile. He was drawing on his repertoire of social skills to get him through an evening with his parents.

Still, we left feeling relieved and hopeful. He had recovered beautifully after his last hospitalization. After some rest and adjustment of medications, he would surely rebound.

On Thursday I woke early with a terrifying sense of uneasiness. The night before, with its happy tableau of Mom, Pop, and Adam watching TV, was a delusion. He wasn't talking. He was awake but still receding from our company. Our evening was a Dilaudid-induced sham, a denial of the true state of things. He wasn't talking!

I rushed to the hospital with mixed feelings of foreboding and optimism—afraid he was dead and half expecting him to be sitting up in bed joking with the nurses.

I found him sleeping, like a man who could wake whenever he felt like it—only now he felt like sleeping.

Overnight, Jenny had transformed the room into their bedroom. She had set about him a few of his favorite books and photographs, including a framed ultrasound image of their unborn daughter, and hung his robe in the closet. She told me he had been taken for an MRI in the middle of the night. After reading the results the resident neurologist had said, "You're too good for us. No surgery for you." Adam had been sleeping ever since, no doubt exhausted by his long day and night.

When he stirred, he nodded to me, and I read him some verses from Psalm 46:

> *God is our refuge and strength,*
> *a very present help in trouble.*
> *Therefore we will not fear, though*
> *the earth should change,*
> *though the mountains shake in*
> *the heart of the sea. . . .*

As always, he accepted words from the Bible, but did he notice that what I read was no longer an assurance of escape but a promise of strength?

Sleeping lightly through the morning, he received nourishment via his IV lines and ate nothing. The few visitors who came seemed shocked by his insensibility to them and left quickly. They spoke to him and asked him questions, to which he replied with an arched eyebrow and a game smile. Sleeping came easy to him, but communication was costing him an enormous effort.

The oncologist and his PA made a brief stop late in the morning to get a DNR—do not resuscitate—directive. Adam motioned them toward Jenny, who agreed not to prolong his life with heroic measures if no improvement was possible. With the agreement secured, they left quickly. He slept on.

Early in the afternoon another priest, not Father David

or Steve, came from Immaculate Conception with the Eucharist. Adam was NPO by that time, so the priest offered him only a crumb of the Eucharist. Adam responded to the Medicine of Immortality exactly the way he had to his first jolt of Dilaudid—with a radiant smile that appeared to say, Thank you, thank you, thank you. His face shone as if he had just been given a glimpse of God. I remembered the psalm verse, "Look to him and be radiant."

By midafternoon, his kidneys were becoming dangerously full, and something would have to be done. His nurse Karen was ready to catheterize him, but he insisted it would not be necessary. All Adam's nurses gave him warm and competent treatment, but Karen added an extraordinary measure of compassion. It came out through her hands with which she touched Adam frankly and lovingly, but even more in the rich timbre of her voice. "Adam," she said with a trace of the Carolina Piedmont in her accent, "let me do this for you."

What followed I can scarcely believe happened. Suddenly Adam threw his legs over the unguarded side of the bed and with the will of an athlete powered his way toward the bathroom. With my shoulder under him and his IV pole in tow, we lurched across the room. How was this possible? Jenny was alarmed by this effort, and Karen knew it was futile. And it was.

While I was out of the room, Karen catheterized him and installed a down drain. When I returned, he was angry with me for failing to stick up for him. In no uncertain terms, he ordered me out of his room.

In the hall outside his room Karen was crying. She felt terrible for Adam and now terrible for Adam's dad. I couldn't help but laugh at how this incident captured so many of our little blowups. It was as if he were a rebellious teenager again and I an unreasonable parent. Those were now the good old days. I told her how delighted I was that he was talking again. I also assured her that he was the most forgiving person I knew. I promised her he would forgive us both.

After a decent interval, I went back into his room.

I took his hand, which had grown shockingly small and soft. "You know, I can't leave you alone," I said.

"*Dad* . . ."—as richly inflected with love as any single word he ever spoke to me.

At mid-evening an assortment of residents, interns, and medical students entered Adam's room in a group. The lights came up, someone vigorously roused Adam, and one of the men in the group began asking him questions in a loud doctor voice, as if shouting over a gale, "Can you tell us your name?"

"Richard Adam Lischer," Adam replied in a voice as clear and commanding as his interrogator's. He spoke his name as if he were testifying in a court of law.

"Do you know where you are?"

"Duke University Medical Center."

"And who is this beautiful young woman beside you?"

Silence. His eye quickly fell on Jenny and then away, but he couldn't speak. It wasn't that he didn't know her; he was too exhausted—or moved—to continue. He seemed profoundly disheartened.

"He knew it last night," I volunteered. "And he knew who was president, too." The point of the game, as I saw it, was to keep asking questions until the patient gets one wrong or, having been humiliated, is reduced to silence.

The procedure had broken me down as well.

The attending physician quickly halted the Q&A and in a few minutes walked out into the hall with me.

"He was a district attorney," I said with some agitation. At first she didn't take my meaning, and, to be honest, neither did I. *He is a man of substance,* I wanted to say. *Do not condescend to this man. Do not say, "Who is this beautiful young woman?" as if he were a senile old man. He is not yours to play with. Do not subject him to this insulting game.*

"He was a district attorney."

"I'm sorry?"

"He was a district attorney. . . ." but louder.

"I understand."

With Jenny's permission, Tracy and I made plans to spend the night with the two of them in Adam's room. Tracy took the recliner; I propped myself between two unyielding square-cut wood and vinyl armchairs beside her; and Jenny did the same at Adam's side.

We were lights-out by 9:30 or 10.

The seizure came within minutes. It seemed even more chaotic and frightening because it happened in the dark and broke violently into our consciousness as we were drifting into sleep.

The room was instantly transformed into a hive of medical activity, with a resident and student on the way, a nurse helping to restrain Adam, and another securing the Ativan and preparing it for injection. Because it began in the darkness, I remember the seizure by the frankness of its sound. It reached its conclusion in the half-light of a small room filled with strangers.

Adam slept on. We tried to settle down in the darkness again, but sleep was impossible for us. Soon another group made a check of Adam, and after they left we turned down the lights once more.

Tracy and I couldn't sleep. The hospital had grown very cold in the night. We found jackets and an extra blanket to throw over us. We walked down the long corridor away from 9300 to a bank of cushioned benches facing the elevators. The place might have been a morgue or a graveyard in the moonlight. We took a little comfort in the dim white lights and in each other's nearness, as we always did. We sat on the cushions under our blanket and shivered.

When we got back to the room, the same medical team was just leaving. Adam had had another seizure in our absence, and Jenny had once again faced it on her own. It was three o'clock in the morning. The three of us arranged our pillows once again and took up our positions. Adam slept on.

Early Friday morning, Jenny hurried home for a shower, and Tracy did the same. By nine o'clock the sun was shining in, and the hospital was no longer a frigid place. Adam was to be moved to a larger room later in the morning. I was sitting at his head, holding his hand, when he had his third seizure in less than twelve hours.

A resident and two nurses came running in and began the usual procedures. The resident was a dark, balding man who, given Adam's cries and my own distress, performed his duty with admirable professionalism. Like the others, this seizure seemed to go on forever, in part because whoever was attending him always had to send someone to *find* the medicine to relieve the seizure. In the meantime, a nurse and I were attempting to comfort and restrain my son, who to my heart was no longer a grown man but a child tormented by terrible dreams. *Hey, sweet boy, it's okay. . . . See, they're gone. Just like that. See?*

At long last it subsided, and the doctor, who had remained so cool under pressure, verifying the dosage and injecting him without so much as a comment or change of expression, and the nurse, who in assisting him had followed her professional code to the letter, wept.

This was the end of Adam for me. These seizures must not continue. Why bring your son to a hospital if they can't stop this wrenching of his soul from his body? Why does it take so long for help to come? Why keep the Ativan in a cabinet? If we can't have our first choice, how about a little peace, and if not peace, why not relief?

As thankful as I was to those who responded to Adam—they were magnificent on 9300—I was angry at the seizures. I was enraged that it was my son who was being raped by cancer and robbed of the consolation prize he had chosen for himself and Jenny. I called his oncologist and asked him to arrange a conference on Adam's treatment. He sent his PA, and by midmorning the PA, two floor doctors, and Tracy, Jenny, and I were standing in the middle of the hall trying to find the balance between keeping Adam alive (for the baby) and relieving his suffering. Meanwhile, his nurse Karen was trying to secure permission for Adam's attendants on each shift to carry Ativan on their person.

In the scramble to get him admitted the doctors appeared

to be working at cross-purposes. I believe his oncologist meant to use the hospital as a hospice, while the staff on 9300 meant to treat him in order to prolong his life. Despairing of the latter, we asked his doctors to make the seizures stop, no matter what.

His oxygen and IV fluids would continue, and the agreement prohibiting heroic measures would remain in place, but now the staff would protect him from seizures with medicines so powerful that they might have the secondary effect of ending his life. Standing there in the hall, we implicitly agreed to cross the line from palliation to the possibility of terminal sedation.

Now when I "see" him in the hospital he is no longer a boy at the mercy of bad dreams but a young man at rest. His body is finally at peace with his spirit. He has settled into his new corner room, a large hexagon at the end of the hall directly across from the nurses' station. The three of us have moved in with him as if we were sharing a hotel room.

Room 9323 is littered with travel bags, pull-along suitcases, and plastic clothing bags. There are also stale Krispy Kremes in their box, newspapers, books, prayer books, and tissues. Two wastebaskets are stuffed with juice empties and paper cups. Cell phones are sitting around with their chargers dangling from outlets. A nurse has been kind enough to bring an aluminum camp bed for Jenny; the junk is piling up on that, too. My shaving equipment and toiletries are set out on the sink along with fresh towels from home. Jenny has rearranged the family photos, including the sonogram of their baby, and placed them around Adam's Bible in a display on the windowsill. How long do we plan on staying?

In the midst of it all, he sleeps on. Graceful in Carolina shorts and a violet t-shirt. Big chest, wide shoulders, pale.

Adam lies rigged in a spiderweb of a dozen wires and tubes, but he no longer seems trapped by them or dependent upon them. They are incidental to his human body. The oxygen line into his nose is looped around each ear; a line from the humidifier keeps his oxygen moist. The hated catheter drops beneath the sheet into a bag below the bed. To his left hangs a blood pressure gauge and to his right a small pump to suction his mouth and a tower of boxes and canisters. The tower sends a single line into each arm carrying saline and Dilaudid with the third reserved for Dilantin if they decide to administer it by drip instead of slow injection. The lines are also pumping Ativan directly toward Adam's brain. The whole venous tangle is connected like Christmas tree lights and plugged into an installed power box.

Two other lines around his neck complete and redeem the picture. One supports the small silver crucifix he bought a few months earlier in Mexico, its tiny figure of Christ frozen in open-armed love for the sterile room and everyone in it; the other is a St. Andrew's Cross from the One World Market on Ninth Street in Durham. They are not incidental to his humanity; even as he sleeps, he is wholly dependent upon them. In these final hours the two paths are moving toward convergence.

The humidifier fills his room with a pleasant gurgle. From somewhere in the tower beside his bed comes a gentle ticking sound and a rhythmic buzz, like a firefly caught between the screen and the window on a summer night. The air conditioner is a constant drone.

This is all we hear. Occasionally, the phone rings but always for someone else. On the intercom startling voices call for other people but never for him. We shift in our chairs and rustle our newspapers. We listen to Adam breathe in perfect rhythm to the gentle respirations of his new environment.

In the afternoon I hear confusing voices from the room next to his. They must belong to a preacher and a nurse. I mentally give them the title "Fugue in a Cancer Ward."

"The age of miracles is not past."
"Can you push on my hand? Go ahead, push. Good!"
"My Jesus says, 'You do not have because you do not ask. And you don't ask because you don't believe.' "
"We're goin' to take a little blood, okay?"
"Oh no, no, no, the age of miracles is not past."
"This little blue one will help you, hon."

On Friday afternoon Jenny decided that Adam should have only family and special visitors. She said to me with more realism than I could bear, "I think Adam is finished speaking to us."

Toward evening we unplugged the phone. Someone posted a NO BLOOD PRESSURE notice, and another, NO NEEDLE STICKS. One of the nurses, a gentle and thoughtful young man, brought in rolls of tape with which he covered the speakers of the intercom. A gift. That night, the charge nurse wrote in her notes that the chances of his "passing" were good, though another nurse, motioning in his direction, said "this" could go on for weeks. *This*.

The four of us again slept all night in 9323.

No seizures.

Jenny remembers that on Saturday Adam was "responsive" to Tracy's whispers and to Sarah's presence. I don't remember this responsiveness. I do recall that he had several visitors, including a student chaplain from the Divinity School. Tracy was not convinced that Adam needed a professional visit, and she warned the young man to be brief and to the point. "If you go in there," she said, "you've got to *give* him something."

He did not seem intimidated by her admonition and entered the room as we left it. A few minutes later I walked past the room with its door ajar. It still moves me when I remember the young man in his white chaplain's coat, kneeling on the floor beside Adam's bed.

In the afternoon Father David and Tom Colley arrived at the same time. Tom waited with us in the hall while David prayed with Adam and Jenny. Tom left us with a photocopy of a printed blessing. When I said that we had no need of it, he insisted, "Oh, no, you keep it."

On Saturday evening the three of us again prepared for night: Tracy in her chair, I in the recliner, Jenny propped and twisted awkwardly on her hip beside Adam, half on her chair, half on his bed. Somehow she managed to hold him tight and lay her head on his pillow without falling between the chair and the bed. She was thirty-eight weeks pregnant. The camp bed remained empty except for a few neatly folded towels and an extra blanket or two.

As we began our sleep, the four of us—I count the baby—were already waiting for the first signs of morning and the gift of a new day. We would endure the night only on condition that it yield us one more dawn.

I remembered the night of his birth, when I couldn't sleep for fear of his dying and Tracy was racked by postoperative nightmares. Now we were waiting again, this time for the first sounds of a seizure. We were sleeping and dreading at the same time, which is what the psalmist must have meant by "the terror of the night."

On Sunday morning we said, "Oh, Jenny, the camp bed was for you. But you didn't use it."

She answered in a soft but firm voice, as if she were a nurse explaining hospital procedure to laypeople. "Last night he needed to feel my breath on his face."

I remembered his promise to help her breathe during labor. She responded by breathing on him through the night.

Then she left to go home for a shower. But before she left she whispered some parting words of permission to Adam. She told him it was okay to let go. She and the baby would be fine. He shouldn't worry. Then she was gone, and it was just the three of us.

There are Sundays when you don't go to church and forget about the holiness of the Lord's Day. Or if you are traveling, you might say to someone, "It doesn't feel like Sunday today, does it?" But on that quiet morning in Adam's room, it *did* feel like Sunday to me. I could imagine acolytes lighting the candles at St. Paul's and Immaculate Conception. I could see the people genuflecting in the aisle, finding their pews, making the sign of the cross, and settling in to pray.

But I could also imagine the freedom of staying in and lingering over a second cup of coffee and the *Times,* the morning sun slanting into the breakfast room, the cat already curled up in her favorite spot.

Adam slept steadily on in his peaceful, Sunday-morning room. His parents might have been roughing it in a rustic cabin in the woods, cramped but comfortable enough. And isn't it always good to be together as a family? Since the boy is sleeping in this morning, the parents speak in hushed tones. Mom is brushing her hair and Dad is shaving at the washbasin. The child does not stir.

And then, at about 8:25, the stillness deepens and something like a shadow moves across the room. With no warning or gasps of distress, it is over.

Since we have not been closely monitoring his sleep, it takes us a few seconds to notice the change in him. I am still standing at the sink when it occurs to me that his gentle respirations have stopped. We move quickly to the bed and watch for his next breath, which never comes. We hold him and speak words of love to him, but he has altogether stopped.

Simultaneously, we began to cry, "Jenny! We've got to call Jenny." At that precise moment, with her name and his ending still suspended in the air, Jenny walked into the room. With hardly a word of explanation, Tracy and I pulled her toward Adam even as we were leaving them to one another.

About five minutes later, she came out into the hall, alone in a way she had never been before, and said to us, "He's gone." The three of us reentered the room and gathered around his bed.

When the nurse returned to his room, we asked her to call the attending physician. He responded promptly and remained long enough to confirm the death. Although I already knew he was dead, to hear the verdict spoken was crushing to us all. The doctor then went out and left the three of us to be with Adam.

This is a scene that never changes.

How gracefully he lies in his shorts and t-shirt, with a sheet draped casually across one of his legs. We remove the oxygen line from his nostrils and unfasten it from his ears. His crosses we will leave in place for the time being.

We pass the better part of an hour remarking upon his beauty. The longer we study him, the finer his nose and mouth appear to us, the more delicate his eyelashes, the stronger his jaw. If he has grown a bit thin in life, now he seems ideally proportioned, with broad shoulders, graceful limbs, and the soft hands of a child, still fit for holding. It appears to us that some artist from antiquity has sanded and polished his skin to perfection. He belongs in a temple. He is not yet a dead body to us but a numen, a spiritual presence in which nothing is wanting but animation.

What a wrenching of love we feel for whatever he now is.

In the blink of an eye, the passions and triumphs of an entire lifetime have vanished into a Sunday morning's dream.

They have mysteriously disappeared into *Adam,* as if his name were an amulet containing all our days. What has happened to them? They are the stuff of yesterday, and now they are no more.

How clean it was. So unlike the messiness of his birth, when we watched him through the glass, turning blue, then yellow, as he contended for life; so unlike the chaos of his admission to this hospital only four days ago when he was suffering and we were begging for mercy. Our prayers have been answered this morning in this, his immaculate ending.

Months later, Paul would tell me that when I called Sarah I couldn't say, "Adam died," but only, "They think Adam died twenty minutes ago," as if his death were a matter of medical dispute. When Sarah arrived, we grieved anew with her, until Room 9323 was bursting with tears.

With Sarah standing beside her brother, Tracy, Jenny, and I took turns reading portions of a blessing over Adam's body. It was the liturgy Tom had left with us. We blessed his beautiful body, his coming in and his going out, and committed his spirit into the hands of the triune God, Father, Son, and Holy Spirit.

We remained with Adam's body for about two hours.

In the meantime, Paul arrived to comfort Sarah. Others stopped by on their way home from church and stood solemnly outside in the hall. Our friend Bill Fulkerson came into the room to be with us.

A man from the hospital arrived to do the paperwork. He asked if we wanted to go to another room, but we said, No, we'll do it here. We talked quietly over Adam, as if he were still sleeping and not to be disturbed.

When it came time to make our good-byes, we did so individually.

Tracy was last because, long ago, she had met him first.

Then we left.

It was noon.

We walked the usual route from the entrance to the medical center along the path we had taken at dawn sixteen months earlier, when he had his surgery to remove the melanoma from his back and he had clean margins and seven chances in ten to survive. We passed employees eating their sandwiches and the smokers on break and walked under the pine trees until we came to the Eye Center parking lot. We pulled a couple of small suitcases with his slippers, sweats, books, and photos in them. Sarah had helped Jenny collect his things and pack them up. Jenny brought his wedding ring and the crosses. The two of them walked close together, comfortable with each other and the silence between them, sisters.

The moment we left the air-conditioned lobby and emerged into the North Carolina heat the world seemed strange to me. What an ugly, disrespectful place it had become, with the clamor of its sirens, ringtones, and shouted conversations. It was as if we had fallen from the realm of the eternal back into time. Everything about our familiar surroundings had changed. That I could not put my finger on the exact nature of the change made me anxious.

When Tracy's mother had a stroke, her eyes were not damaged, but something in her visual cortex never allowed her to see the world as she once had. It took me less than a minute to feel that way too.

When Tracy and I got home, we drove up the long gravel road from which we would never be confronted by the mound of someone we loved. We passed the low-branched Climbing Tree, and for a moment I mislaid the generations and imagined that little Adam had once climbed in it. A cloud of dust followed us most of the way and then loitered like a pall in the still air above the meadow.

You are dust, and unto dust you shall return.

The house did not look familiar to me.

Without a word, we got out of the car and knelt in the planted beds by the driveway and mindlessly began to pull up the chickweed from among the dead stalks and wilted flowers. As dry and unpromising as it was, the dirt felt good in our hands.

15

In his "Funeral Blues" W. H. Auden wrote,

> *Stop all the clocks, cut off the telephone,*
> *Prevent the dog from barking with a juicy bone,*
> *Silence the pianos and with muffled drum*
> *Bring out the coffin, let the mourners come.*

The funeral begins the moment he dies. Even for those, like us, who relinquished control of time, who prayed, *I wait for the Lord,* and who begged for nothing more than one more dawn—even for the likes of us, death introduces its own brand of motion rather than stillness. For the momentum that propels you forward is not fueled by his absence, but by his presence. He is still a part of your life-world. Your love for him will not rest.

Someone has to help him decide on the relative merits

of Taxol versus Avastin. Someone has to shadow him like a bodyguard from clinic to clinic. Someone has to write love letters to him and kiss the top of his head. Someone has to set the table on family occasions. Someone has to iron his shirts. Someone has to find a new place for him to live. Someone has to keep watch with him for the morning. Your responsibilities to him have not ended.

It takes awhile to realize that you have been demoted to a lesser intensity of time and to a less urgent order of duties. Everything still matters, of course, but not as much as it did yesterday. Each hour no longer swells with the fullness of meaning as it did when he was struggling to remain alive. How much better it would have been to set aside one of the days between his death and the funeral to pray and keep silence.

By two p.m. on Sunday we were meeting with the priest and the funeral director in Jenny's living room. Later in the afternoon, Jenny, her mother Alice, Tracy, and I were walking the graves at St. Matthew's Cemetery, trying to decide between an open view of the sky or a place beside some trees but a bit nearer the lane than we would have liked. Jenny chose the trees.

When we returned from the cemetery, our old friends Dennis and Leesa Campbell were waiting for us in our kitchen, having hurried down from Charlottesville when they heard the news.

When we drove up our driveway, we didn't recognize their car even with its Virginia plates. Tracy said, "I hope these are friends."

Shortly after they left, I went upstairs to my study to write Adam's obituary.

"Richard Adam Ewers Lischer, of Durham, died Sunday morning, July 17, after a brief struggle with cancer. He was 33.

"He was the husband of Jennifer Lischer, to whom he was married in 1999 and who sustained him throughout his illness, and the father of a baby girl whose birth is soon expected."

In the obituary, I mentioned his faithfulness at daily Mass; I should have added the more declarative "He died believing in God."

From the day of his second diagnosis Adam lived exactly thirteen and a half weeks. That is the equivalent of an astronomic quarter. On earth it is a spring or an autumn complete; in a woman's womb, a trimester; in school, one academic semester. In the church's reckoning of time, it is the precise distance from Ash Wednesday to Pentecost, from the day of dust to the day of fire. It was Adam's final season. Today he completed it.

When I finished the obituary, I deleted his name and number from my cell phone.

That night, when Tracy and I couldn't sleep, we made our first joined response to Adam's passing. Our reaction was bedrock Bach: *Come, Sweet Death*. We felt we had been given secret knowledge of the sort that is available to everyone but grasped by only the few. We had been initiated into an open secret. And what is that special knowledge? Everyone must die.

We saw a vast company of spirits joined in a common dance, but it was not horrible or frightening, only natural. Every person in that enormous hospital, everyone at the malls and on TV, all our friends, including Dennis and Leesa, Tom and Father David, our young Jenny and Sarah, and—oh, my God, even Lukey and Calvin—all of them will die. Sitting on top of the covers at one in the morning, we suspended the hierarchical view of the generations and saw ourselves and those we love as a vast field of lights, every single one of which must go out. They may not go out in the expected order or in the same manner, but they will go out. We live only in the flicker created by their random dying. What we had known of death intellectually, we now possessed as a triumphant certainty. In the wee hours of July 17–18 it was the only absolute truth available to us.

Now that we understood the mystery of death, we were welling with admiration for our son. He had finished his job and accomplished his mission, the necessity of which was now clear to us. Everything he had striven for in his life was not canceled by death but fulfilled in our presence this very morning. And so cleanly, with such an absence of desperation. An added mercy, to be sure. The cancer in the brain took him quickly before it ravaged his body. He *was* gorgeous, wasn't he?

Such thoughts would evaporate by Monday morning's light. They were nothing more than the first cheap tricks grief plays on the bereaved. It sends its victims good and reasonable consolations in the form of universal truths and congratulatory telegrams. It encourages survivors to ponder the immensity of time and to think on a geologic scale and not the human one in which the loss of years or even a few days has the power to rip your heart in two.

What you don't get on that very first night is true *bereavement,* which is the chill of absence that goes to the bone, like the shock of walking into a meat locker on a summer's afternoon. What you don't get is the one-two punch of *It cannot be / It is,* whose order of blows alternates with surprising playfulness. What you cannot experience on the first night are the never-ending waves of longing. It will be a day or two before it all begins to set in. When it does, nothing will be good, and nothing will make sense, and nothing will help. C. S. Lewis wrote of his own grief, "If I knew any way of escape I would crawl through sewers to find it."

Adam's oak casket was brought to the church on Tuesday afternoon. Several employees of Immaculate Conception told me that the light streaming through the south and west windows created a spectacular, prismatic effect above him as he was placed before the altar in the main sanctuary. They said they had never seen anything like it. I understand the springs of such testimonies, but for me it was too late for a God-wink of the miraculous.

On Tuesday night hundreds of people stood in line to greet Jenny, who was seated in an armchair in the narthex of Immaculate Conception. Sarah stood by her side the whole evening and greeted visitors. Tracy spoke with friends in another corner of the large gathering space just beneath the large, Protestant-style stewardship banner: Tiempo, Talento, Tesoro.

I had asked Adam's friend Jason Harrod to play some of his own blues and bluegrass compositions as people waited patiently to pay their respects. He sat in the gathering space near the entrance to the main sanctuary, strumming his guitar and humming some of Adam's favorites.

> *When I fly away, I will be unbound.*
> *When I fly away, I'm nowhere to be found. . . .*
>
> *When I fly away through the heat and cold,*
> *When I fly away, I will not grow old. . . .*
>
> *When I fly away, I won't be afraid.*
> *When I fly away, I will be remade.*

I stood in the sanctuary a few feet up the aisle from the casket. There was a candle burning at each side of it. Many who came knelt at the base of the catafalque and used the coffin as an altar for prayer.

When you stand in the mourner's line, your whole life reanimates itself; its characters return to say hello, hold your hand, or touch your face. It was as if they had come out of the scrapbooks and albums in our storage room to be with us once again. All the playmates from the old neighborhood reappeared, along with their parents. How did they get so gray?

Young men and women introduced themselves as if they were ground troops come to honor the fallen drum major, as if they had gone into battle with him only yesterday, and not fifteen years before.

"I was a trumpet in the marching band."

"Flute, Mr. Lischer."

"Baton."

"Tuba."

"Snare."

On Wednesday morning at ten o'clock Adam's casket was moved from the Daily Mass Chapel, where he and Jenny had knelt every morning beneath the San Damiano Cross, and placed at the rear of the main sanctuary. With the prelude finished, the congregation stood and turned to face the processional cross. The funeral Mass was about to begin. You could have heard a pin drop in the enormous sanctuary.

At that moment we symbolically reversed the laborious plot of Adam's ninety-five days. Tracy, Jenny, Sarah, and I each held a corner of the cream-colored linen pall with a purple cross emblazoned at its center. The cross was trimmed in rose, for joy. We unfolded it and covered the bare casket with it, as if we were making a bed or tucking a child in for the night. What had been stripped and exposed like the altar on Maundy Thursday, we dressed again. We carefully placed the pall over his coffin with the cross above his chest. Once again he was arrayed in fine cloth as he had been at his baptism.

Then the congregation began to sing "Lift High the Cross," and the funeral procession was under way.

In his homily, Father David beautifully captured Adam's personality and faith. The priest's eyes crinkled under white eyebrows when he spoke of his "easy, natural, wry humor. It was one of his many human touches that put you at ease," he continued, "and endeared you to the man, and him to you."

He testified to Adam's devotion to the daily sacrament at

Immaculate Conception and then added, "The jewel that was his Lutheran faith simply had another setting in God's providential plan."

To Jenny he had this to say: "Loving him with strength and courage, dignity and grace, you gave him life. You helped to make his living and his dying a song. It was plaintive, classical, romantic, and soul-searing. Only you know the depth of it."

You gave him life. I remembered how he promised to help her breathe during labor, and how, thirty-eight weeks into her pregnancy, she responded by breathing into his face on the last night of his life.

Then I thought of the baby waiting to be born.

There are those who say the sermon is a relic of a bygone era. It is passé and largely irrelevant to the contemporary life of faith. I can only reply that by the end of the day, when we finally had a moment to talk, Tracy and I had, independent of one another, memorized several passages from Father David's lyrical homily.

"Because of Adam's great love—his love of Jenny and his family, his love of friends and colleagues, and yes, his great love of those he served through the law, especially those sentenced to death—all the love that characterized his life threw him into the arms of love itself forever.

"We have not lost this good Christian man, Adam Lischer. Nor do we consign him merely to the faulty memory of human history. We join together in our hope that God is ever faithful to God's promises. God always promises life. Adam now lives with God, never to die again. May he rest in peace."

Then the congregation sang "On Eagle's Wings."

Before the commendation, David solemnly walked around the casket and censed it with burning spices and gums. Their bittersweet aroma filled the chancel. The incense did not purify Adam, but it was an outward sign of the purity he had achieved at great cost. I did not know the incense was coming, but as we watched the smoke rise toward the cross and dissipate into the space above it, it seemed the truest gesture of the day. Once again, amidst the last lingering wisps of his purification, I was very proud of Adam.

The funeral cortege took us through the familiar neighborhoods of northern Durham and Orange County. To view the old schoolyards and practice fields through the tinted windows of a black Fleetwood Brougham creates another perceptual disruption.

We took the very road (heading north instead of south) on which Adam and I had hitched a ride after our ill-fated canoe trip twenty-three years earlier. We passed the ruins of the country store where the pair of loopy Good Samaritans had dropped us off. The remains of the lean-to porch are still there too, where we waited for Tracy to come and get us. We even crossed a few of the streets on our old paper route—the one we got fired from on January 28, 1986, the day Adam had pneumonia and the *Challenger* blew up.

He and Sarah learned to drive on these roads. There, near that intersection—it could have been that very culvert—he skidded in the snow and put a permanent crease in my new Subaru, and Tracy said to him (and me), "Oh, honey, it's only a car."

The more familiar the places, the more displaced I felt on our journey to his final resting place.

Nine-year-old Adam would have enjoyed the ride in the big black car. That's how old he was when we buried my father. I remember Adam rode shotgun next to the driver and nearly wore him out kibitzing about the "Caddie" with the two-way radio. "How does it work? Do you say 'Over and out' or 'Ten-four'?"

This time it would have been the motorcycles. Because he had been a prosecutor, he got a police escort on motorcycles. They darted in and out of the procession like bumblebees. He got along exceedingly well with policemen; a day spent with his investigator was, as far as he was concerned, a day of high adventure.

As we turned into the cemetery, the policemen lined up their cycles and stood beside them to form an honor guard for the hearse. He would have thought that was funny. But he would have loved it.

For me, however, the service had already ended in the clouds of incense.

In the noontime heat Tom and Father David read through the committal quickly. "Into your hands, Father of mercies, we commend our brother Adam in the sure and certain hope that, together with all who have died in Christ, he will rise with him on the last day."

Then the mortuary distributed a long-stemmed rose to each member of the family to lay across Adam's coffin. Tracy and I weren't prepared for this gesture of sentimentality; for us the pall with its purple cross had been enough.

The incense in the church seemed right because it signifies

immolation with a remainder distilled from it. Something, or someone, is sacrificed, but its substance has been transformed and remains. The roses seemed out of place because roses only camouflage the smell of rotting flesh. With the incense you get purification. The roses are a cover-up.

Except for a stray image or two, the rest of the day has disappeared from memory, like the smoke from the incense or the last ringing chords of the final hymn. At the gathering at our house afterward, Tracy picked up little Calvin, born six months earlier on Adam's birthday, and kept him in her grip for the entire afternoon, as if he were her personal flotation device. He held on to his grandmother for dear life and kept his face buried in her neck. The child was no longer Baby Calvin but Baby Adam, and my wife had mastered our new truth: everybody at this party dies.

Nine days after the funeral, we got a call from an exhausted but jubilant widow. Jenny was on the line, phoning from a more cheerful wing of Duke Medical Center. In a voice that reminded me of Adam's way of delivering good news, she said, "*Hey,* Rick. I just [*just!*] wanted to let you know that you have a new granddaughter.

"Her name is [*pause, beat*—Adam would have been proud of her timing]—*Elizabeth Adam.*"

With Adam's wedding ring on her thumb, his picture by her bed, and his St. Andrew's Cross around her neck, she had delivered their baby girl. As per Adam's request, Sarah had stood in for him and coached her through a long and difficult labor.

Just before Jenny called us, she laid the child across her own body, peered into her bunched face and searching eyes, and solemnly named her. "You are Elizabeth Adam," she said.

Elizabeth followed hard upon her father's death in the same hot July and the same summer of our shattered dreams. The little troupe reassembled on the old stage, the taste of ashes still in our mouths, and the same weary actors traded their laments for tears of joy. Duke Medical Center, of all places, once a scene of suffering and death, had become a place of resurrection.

Who could have imagined Jenny's resiliency? Her ability to smile? And our Sarah—a grieving labor coach? Who would have thought anything resembling *joy* could follow our night of weeping?

Who would have guessed a baby with hair like Bon Jovi?

It's as if we all needed a learner's permit in order to live one more day on the planet.

Elizabeth Adam emerged from the womb with dark, spiked hair and an attitude. "Deal with it," she seemed to say. She will be no one's consolation prize for a dead father. She will be her own weeping, sleeping, sucking, and pooping little person.

The child has most of her mother's features and, now that her spiked hair has lightened up and settled down, she looks even more like Jenny, the strawberry blond. When she laughs her nose crinkles as her mother's still does, and her blue eyes dance like her father's. She has her father's broad mouth and his clean-clefted upper lip. If you are quick enough with the camera, you may catch the vulnerability of her father too, that of a little boy trying to be good but not always succeeding. In

Elizabeth Adam, her mother's sweet reserve coexists with her father's open-throttled lack of it, all in one sturdy package.

Elizabeth is powerful testimony to our dogged belief in Platonic Ideas. We were so preoccupied with the child's pre-existence that when she was finally born it was as if we had known her in another life. She was *the* context of everything that happened during her father's ninety-five days. After his death "How's that baby?" became the shorthand expression for all the sorrows and joys that had visited our family. Most of our fantasies—Adam's coaching Jenny through the delivery, Adam proudly holding her at her baptism—had to be discarded, as did Jenny's more desperate scenario: her mother would live upstairs with the baby while Jenny camped out on the lower level and cared for her dying husband. None of these outcomes materialized on July 29, 2005, except one: Elizabeth Adam.

On the day Adam was hospitalized for the last time, Tom Colley said that birth and death belong together as transitions to very different orders of life. Under the circumstances, these sentiments sounded a little smooth to me. We assumed that Adam's funeral would conclude one dispensation and his daughter's birth would begin another, as if they belonged to entirely different narratives. But Tom was right; at some primal level the two events could not be separated, and Jenny didn't try. The St. Andrew's Cross that ushered Adam into the next world welcomed Elizabeth into this one. His departure and her arrival were marked by fearful pangs and cries and a leap into the unknown.

The Caves

16

Before Adam died I had a theory of grief. It was not original, and I shared it with my family. I told them our "grief work" had already begun during the final months of Adam's life as we came to terms with the terminal nature of his illness. I spoke of grief as if it were a jail sentence that could be reduced by time already served in the ER, the cafeteria, and at his bedside, places where so much of our sadness had already played itself out. I came close to suggesting that we might skip the purgatory of anger, longing, and depression and go straight to blessedness.

My theory of grief proved to be untrue. It was another false lead, like our high-altitude view of life and death in the waning hours of that first night. It was a fine tactic for coping with our son's dying, but it had nothing to do with his death.

Only after he was gone did we fully appreciate the qualitative distinction between illness and absence, the chasm between *terminal* and *terminated*. Only after Adam died did we realize we had not been grieving at all, for grief is longing for one who is absolutely unattainable. We had been swarming like moths around a flickering candle, but it was still giving off a little light.

On the day he died Sarah said to her mother, "I wanted to spend the whole day with him." It no longer mattered to her that he wasn't communicating with us. In the absence of his ability to perform the most rudimentary tasks, the substance of him remained—a permanent bed for his vanishing attributes. I understand why some families can't pull the plug on the loved one who is lingering in a vegetative state. There is someone *there* to spend the day with, someone who is greater than the sum of his deficits. In those last days we were coping with the anguish that precedes death, but we had not begun to grieve.

Only with the extinguishing of the light comes the True Darkness.

Grief is a series of caves—dark, multiple, and unfathomed. You do not explore them. You fall into them. Which means you are constantly righting yourself and daily, sometimes hourly, recovering from little plunges into unrequited longing and despair.

Grief bears witness to no story larger than itself. It shrinks your life and daily interactions to the exact size of your longing. Your world is not as large as it used to be, for a ceiling has been imposed on happiness and the floor occasionally trembles beneath your feet. It's a snug fit—you and your sadness, you and your resentment, you and your self-pity. Tracy was feeling it when she described her grief as "a layer of fat that encircles your entire body and smothers you."

Two of the characters in Peter De Vries' *The Blood of the Lamb,* each of whom is the father of a terminally ill child, discuss the horrific effects of cancer treatment on their children. One of the fathers says,

"But that's medicine, the art of prolonging disease."
"Jesus," I said, with a laugh. "Why would anybody want to prolong it?"
"In order to postpone grief."

Within a few weeks of Adam's death, a new dimension of grief began to make its appearance: I was clearly losing the sense of my son's presence, and it terrified me. When I woke the morning after he died, I could still feel him in my space, the way a blind person senses the presence of an invisible other. That first morning he and I still occupied the same physical plane; the early sun might well have cast two shadows across the bedroom floor instead of one. But now his near palpable relevance to my world was slipping away, and I couldn't do anything about it. I wore his cross and t-shirts and haunted his old hangouts, but he continued to take evasive action. Hardly anyone talked to me about him or acknowledged his absence; it was as if he were a sensitive topic, about which the less said the better.

There is no word in a Western language for the parent of a dead child. It's as if the languages of the West have entered into a conspiracy of silence about "this horrible club," as a friend who lost a child called it. The silence is peculiar, not only because such grief deserves a name, but also because it changes the nature of marriage itself. "Let me into your grief," the man begs his wife in Frost's poem, if only to break the silence between them. The parents will always know terrible things that others can only imagine or fear.

Tracy is sitting in the corner of the breakfast room with her legs curled under her and a glass of wine in her hand. She is gazing toward the meadow at a long view of nothing. "What are you thinking about?"

She looks at me as if to say, You have to ask?

I find myself attending Masses in Adam's memory whenever they are held, not because I believe the dead need our prayers or his soul is in limbo, but because I long to hear his name spoken aloud in the world of the living: "Of your charity, please pray for the repose of the soul of Adam Lischer." In that moment, nowhere else on the planet does the sound of him fill the same air that I breathe.

It was and continues to be a standoff between two implacable realities: love, which makes a dead man achingly present in the midst of an ordinary day; and time, which renders the same man irrelevant. No wonder the psalmist complained, "I have passed out of mind like one who is dead."

Just as I was losing touch with Adam, Tracy was being blessed night after night by visions, epiphanies, and sweet dreams. In one of them she dreamed that Adam walked into our house in the middle of the afternoon, as usual without knocking. He wore a white shirt of gauze, and his face was so cleanly scrubbed it gave off light. She asked him, "Are you able to come here and do this because you are so spiritual?" to which he responded with a bemused look but remained silent. He walked from room to room, looking at everything very carefully with no apparent urgency or purpose. Tracy thought to show him the child asleep in her crib. Adam studied her intently and then with a half smile walked away and out of the house. He didn't seem amazed by his child's beauty; it was as if he had seen her before

"And it wasn't just a dream," she insists.

For my part, I would have welcomed any of my weird dreams, but they had deserted me entirely. I could only envy my wife, who couldn't wait to go to sleep at night.

I called Bill Coffin, who advised me to "talk to him," the way he talked to his Alex, but that didn't work for me.

I spoke with Father David, who intensified Bill's advice by remarking, almost casually, that he prayed to Adam as an intercessor. That got my attention. He patiently explained to me that Adam was now more like God than like us. The dead are completed beings who are no longer subject to the limitations of time and space and are therefore available to us across the entire surface of our lives. "Their angels," Jesus says, "always behold the face of my Father."

"Remember what Augustine called eternity? He called it 'Today.' Think of the possibilities for communion," he said to me, his stunned and grateful audience. I listened carefully.

Late one afternoon, while Tracy and I sat on a bench with a long view of Adam's grave among the maple and sycamore trees in the distance, I confessed to her, "I can't feel him out there anymore."

She said, "Don't worry about that. If you can't go to him, let him come to you."

Then in late October 2005, on the very day Tracy left Durham for a trial in another city, something new happened. The scar tissue from an old surgery finally closed around my lower intestine, and I couldn't move for pain. I called Tom and he drove me to the ER at Duke Medical Center.

Counting the emergencies with Bob, Nina, and Adam, it was my tenth trip to the ER in six months, but this time it was me. When they wheeled me into the lobby and I caught sight of the armed guards, the metal detectors, the turnstile, and the chaos of suffering in that crowded room, I wept for the members of our family who had passed through these same portals, for Adam most of all, and I wept for myself.

Two nights after emergency surgery, I woke up alone in a corner room of Duke Medical Center, the same room he had occupied, but two floors below. It was about eleven p.m. I was in terrific pain with a six-inch incision up my gut, heavily medicated, and disoriented to the point of psychosis. I both knew and did not know where I was.

I believed that I was the leading character in an Edward Albee teleplay that was being staged in the hospital or in a built replica of the hospital. Many people were watching me, but I couldn't see them. The playwright had ingeniously incorporated my room and the corridor outside my room into his set. The nurses and technicians were actors with makeup and perfect hair. I could tell by how quickly my nurse translated Celsius into Fahrenheit that she was not a real nurse.

After she left, I painfully got out of bed and cracked the door open onto the hall. The light in the hall was blinding, obviously the result of supplementary lighting for the production. That Albee is a genius, I thought. He manages everything, but he himself never appears. I crawled back into bed with unformed feelings of anxiety, paranoia, and wonder. I waited for developments. After a few minutes, I got out of bed again and dragged myself into the corner bathroom. I was looking for the camera and also a safe room where I couldn't be watched or filmed, where the director-god could not observe me.

I didn't find the camera in there, but I did find my son. He did not appear to me as an apparition, but he came to me as a memory so powerful that it verged on presence. I remembered our ridiculous attempts to remove his gowns without detaching his IV in a bathroom exactly like this one—same tiled walls and fixtures—minus, I presume, the hidden cameras. I could see the color of his skin and feel his body, his soft hands, and the muscles in his forearms.

Late into the evening and throughout the night, a great hospital makes its sounds. At first they vie with one another for attention, but ultimately they combine in a single murmur. Nurses and orderlies chat and laugh quietly among themselves. Breathing machines sigh as if burdened by the life they are supporting. Monitors buzz on officiously and occasionally bleat like startled birds. Bags of fluid drip and tick to their own rhythm. Once you actually *hear* the fluorescent lights, their hum is as deafening as the roar of cicada or the noise of test patterns. I had listened to the whole perverted symphony only four months before.

One of the sounds I heard on the corridor that night, not quite lost among the others, was the voice of my son. He called to me softly from the heart of the night and said nothing at all, as if wanting only to let me know he was there.

What I experienced was not a dream. It was a hospital-acquired epiphany. Not the meeting I yearned for, but beggars can't be choosers. I came closer to a physical encounter with Adam that night than I had since the day he died.

I hauled myself back into bed, readjusted the guardrail, and dialed my home telephone number, not knowing what to expect. What I needed now was the one necessary voice. When Tracy answered, I told her what had happened to me and asked, "Am I dreaming?"

She said, "You are, darling, you are. Go back to sleep."

17

If I make my bed in hell, you are there.
—Psalm 139:8b

In the weeks following Adam's death, Tracy and I reread Dietrich Bonhoeffer's *Letters and Papers from Prison*. I had studied the *Letters* as a graduate student in theology, but this time we read them together as an end-of-life narrative, as the story of a young man in his midthirties who is trying to come to terms with the loss of his own future. We read them in the same spirit with which Adam explored his own illness: not so much for help in coping, but for their insights into God's role in our suffering. This was especially important to me, who had replaced my prayer book with an unabridged dictionary.

We understood that resisting illness is not the same as resisting Hitler, and living with cancer is not the same as life in a concentration camp, but we were both moved by an underlying similarity between Bonhoeffer's faithfulness and our son's. There is a current running through his letters that sounded familiar to us: it is the stripping of altars, the inexorable reduction of life to its touchstone. That was Adam's plot too.

In Bonhoeffer we could hear the titanic struggle between survival and nothingness that went on in Adam. Already in the spring of 1943 he wrote a friend, "I sometimes feel as if my life were more or less over. . . . But, you know, when I feel like this, there comes over me a longing (unlike any other that I experience) to have a child and not to vanish without a trace—"

By January 1945, he had adopted a fully retrospective view of his own life. He made the telltale gesture of instructing his parents to give away all his clothes, including the salt-and-pepper suit and the brown shoes. According to the witness of the prison doctor, before he went to the gallows Bonhoeffer removed his prison clothes and knelt in prayer. On April 9, 1945, the stripping of his altar was completed.

In the summer of Adam's death, the letter we returned to most frequently was dated Christmas Eve 1943. In it, Bonhoeffer writes wistfully of the *gap* that separates friends from one another by distance or death. He says that most people assume—mistakenly—that it is God's job to fill in the gap with compensations, perhaps in the form of inspiring thoughts, diversions, or false expectations. Not so, he insists. In fact, the opposite is true. God keeps the gap *open* between us and those we love, "even at the cost of pain." I later found a similar view of grief in one of Freud's letters in which he reflects on the death of his adult daughter Sophie: "No matter what may fill the gap, even if it be filled completely, it nevertheless remains something else. And actually this is how it should be. . . . It is the only way of perpetuating that love which we do not want to relinquish."

"Parents of murdered children seeking closure," the newspaper headline proclaims without a hint of irony. Sure they are. Along with "moving on" or "turning the page," "closure" tops the hit parade of clichés oppressing the bereaved. "Closure" paves over the craters and cankers in the gap; it locks doors that, for the time being, should be left ajar. In our case, not only would closure suppress honest feelings of grief, but it would deny the love that made grief possible in the first place.

The truth is, we are all creatures of the gap, living out our days between the giddy promises of youth and the inevitability of death. What we find there is not resolution, but multiple contradictions. And religious believers are no more immune to them than anyone else.

Believers confess that God is good; yet, like everyone else, we live with losses no one in his right mind would call "good." It will never be "good" in any spiritual sense that Adam never brushed his daughter's hair, never read *Goodnight Moon* to her, and was not permitted, even once, to sit by her bed and study her while she sleeps. It will never be good for them to be apart. Far from defending God's goodness, C. S. Lewis admitted, "Sometimes it is hard not to say 'God forgive God.'"

What Bonhoeffer adds to the paradox, however, changes the believer's experience of life in the gap: we live with these contradictions in companionship with God, who makes up for his many failures by sharing in our suffering. Bonhoeffer wrote, "I don't want to go through this affair without faith." When Tracy and I read that, we thought of Adam, who felt the same way about his ordeal.

A Jewish mystic said, "The more I know what God is not, the more I know about God." "God" is *not* a synonym for security or happiness, a cipher for success. That god is an idol. Instead, we should be content to live as if God were absent or, as Bonhoeffer said, not a "given" (which is often the experience of those who suffer)—but always by faith in the One who is mysteriously present.

Believers often give God an excused absence by referring to his "transcendence," as if it were a condition, like rheumatism, which would explain why he seems so feeble and remote from our lives: God is so far above us that we can't relate to him nor he to us. But there is another kind of transcendence, based not on distance but convergence, which cancels out the traditional metaphor and ushers God into the world of homeless shelters, prison cells, cancer wards, and the human heart itself. God is so transcendently *close* we cannot see him, and so woven into the fiber of things that he remains hidden, like the key that is "lost" in plain view. In the Beatitudes, Jesus offers a clue to God's whereabouts in the world: look for God in the poor, the persecuted, the dying, and those who mourn.

I remember our shopping trip to the mall and our Father's Day outing at the ball game, when I watched my son moving slowly and in evident pain. At first, it helped me to imagine him in the company of a friend. It was the gaunt Man of Sorrows himself who was *with* him, like a gnarled cane or a walker supporting him in the passage from life to death. But as things grew more intense I began to see Jesus *in* him, as if he and Adam were doing the Stations together and the two of them had agreed to share a single, broken body.

I can still hear the shrill voice from the hospital room next to his: *The age of miracles is not past.* But now we know it is a different miracle than the one we dreamed about in the summer of 2005. Not the supernatural escape from illness, but the faithful companion in the Valley. Not the restored flesh we hoped for, but God in the flesh of those who suffer.

That's why we loved Adam's flesh—the graceful body with its underlying sinewy strength, but also the small tumors on his side and his pale white head—because what his body was losing in mass it was gaining in transparency. The sacred presence had always been there, of course, as it is in each of us, like stars on a cloud-filled night, but we had never seen it so clearly as when he began to die.

As long as we continue to eat and drink in community, we will never plug up the gap that separates us from our son, for every meal reminds us of how little self-sufficiency we can claim for ourselves and how dependent we are on others for nourishment. That's the way it was in the summer of 2005, and that's the way it is today. I remember how like a patriarch he presided at our dining table, covered with the signature dishes of friends and strangers, in a room so filled with love you could taste its saltiness. At the table where he said, "Tee it up, big guy," and we recited "Come Lord Jesus" like children. I remember our family's last supper at Adam and Jenny's house with boxes of Colonel Sanders on the table. I remember his first communion when he was twelve and his last Eucharist on an adjustable tray in Room 9323 and the many tables that came between. I remember thousands of meals prepared by Tracy in "Peggy's Restaurant," including waffles every Sunday night, and the many graces spoken in unison at our family table. I remember the long table by the Potomac in Washington, D.C., when we raised our glasses to him and celebrated half the night. I remember our breakfast in the diner with a U-Haul parked outside. I remember the day of his baptism and the banquet of fried chicken, tortellini soup, and beer that followed. I remember the buffet after his funeral, paid for by the love of a friend.

All our meals belong to the open space in the gap, because we are never really finished with eating. We are never so full of love for one another that we don't need to share a meal, and we are never so full of God that we don't need him to feed us with bread and wine. When it comes to this sort of nourishment, Adam once asked, can there ever be "too much"?

I *think* about Adam a lot when I am alone, but I most often *meet* him at a table with others. That's where Jesus met his friends too, at a table, where he was determined to be something other than history to them. When I approach the altar for Communion, the many meals of our lives coalesce into one. By faith, I sense another room, another table, another source of light, and join the feast in progress. The table is always dressed in white or gold as if for Easter. It reflects the glory of the Host who presides in our midst but never makes an appearance.

Adam is there too, as he was in our bedroom the morning after his death or during my hallucinatory night in the hospital. Then his presence was nearly palpable but marred by the aftershocks of death. Now his reality is no less powerful but in a more relaxed and companionable way. He is not tied down by oxygen lines, infusion bags, and the paraphernalia of suffering. Of all that he is blessedly free. He is no longer the man of dust we baptized and buried, but a child of perpetual light.

In the time it takes to kneel in an ordinary church, the company of those who had a hand in composing *Adam,* as well as those whose lives he touched, are gathered together for food and drink. We are in communion—but elusively so. From our perspective, we come and go, but for Adam it is different. He is no longer encumbered by sequence, schedule, and the need to be in the right place at the right time. Father David was right. He is present to God and we are present to him all the time.

I eat the scrap of bread, drink the wine, and then linger for a few seconds with Tracy, and sometimes Elizabeth, before tearing myself away from the table.

The service often ends with the prayer "that we may be one with all the saints." Then we all leave the sanctuary and return to the clock and the day at hand.

The theologian Karl Barth once remarked, "God is so unassuming in the world," which may be the *only* way those who grieve experience the presence of God. Nobody's grief is characterized by sudden movements or dramatic reversals. Grief does not "break" like a fever.

I was reading some of the same psalms Adam and Jenny read before he died, more as a method of staying in touch with him than seeking a spiritual blessing. I noticed that in most of them the figure of God is bathed in light; but Psalm 139 strays from the familiar imagery by asking the reader to imagine that light and darkness are the same to God. If true, it means that God is capable of working in the dark. Which means that healing begins where creation began: in chaos and darkness. God doesn't wait until the depression lifts or spiritual adjustments have been made before he begins to stir in the human heart. That afternoon in the cemetery when Tracy said, "Let him come to you," she was referring to Adam—"him"—but I later realized she was also talking about God. There is nothing you can do: let Him come to you.

A few weeks after the funeral we took our grandson Luke to the beach, just the three of us. We stayed up late watching movies, eating Klondike Bars, and listening to the ocean. We turned out all the lights and lost ourselves in *E.T., The Lion King,* and *Willie Wonka and the Chocolate Factory.* It came as something of a shock to Tracy and me that we could laugh out loud *and* grieve our lost son at the same time. Other bereaved parents may come to the same realization in the enjoyment of music, sex, or work. We found it first with Luke and Willie Wonka. We began to realize, even then, that other loves would form a supporting web of new tissue and cartilage around his irreplaceable loss. At some level, Luke understood that we were treating him as our new little boy. He accepted the role and played it to sweet perfection.

I later traveled to Indianapolis to give three lectures at a conference for newly ordained ministers. It was late in the evening of my second presentation, and I was more than ready to get back to my hotel room. A young black man named Marcus who had been waiting his turn in a small group of students finally approached me.

"Dr. Lischer, I've been waiting to ask you one question."

"Okay, shoot."

"How's Adam?"

Who? Do I know an Adam?

It's much easier to take a body blow if you have time to tense the muscles in your stomach. Then you say, "Now."

"I was a student at Wesley Seminary while Adam was attending American Law School next door. We lived in the same building."

Oh, *that* Adam.

"I was going through a rough time back then," the young man said. "I wasn't sure the ministry was for me. The money wasn't there and my bills were piling up. When I met Adam I had already decided to quit. We played basketball every evening that fall, just the two of us, behind the apartments—one-on-one in the dark." He laughed at the thought of it. "It was Adam who told me not to give up and not to quit. He always said I would make a great pastor. He told me that every night. I never forgot it. So—what's he doing?"

I had a flashback to a mellow 2-L who was never so overburdened by studies that he couldn't hang out with a friend, especially on an asphalt basketball court. I could see him in his baggy shorts and sweatshirt with the sleeves cut off, no t-shirt underneath despite the chill in the autumn air. The baseball cap is backwards, of course, and later tossed aside as the scrimmage grows more intense. Finally, his voice: high, clear, and positive, assuring his friend that he belongs in the ministry. "If that's your calling, man, you should do it."

I already knew he was an optimist with a gift for encouraging others, but it was exhilarating to be reminded. My son considered me a hopeless pessimist, doomed by a lethal mix of Germanic genes and Lutheran theology. As a teenager he once created a file on my computer and bookmarked it for me: "Dad's Problems." He himself had the mind of a Catholic and the heart of a Methodist. One year for Christmas he gave me a book by a famous motivational speaker and forged the author's signature along with the inscription, "To Rick, always do your best!" I have since found two other books on my shelves, both gifts from him and both with the same inscription. The odd thing is, when I read these forgeries again, I actually *do* try to do my best.

When the nightwatchman at Tracy's office looks me in the eye and says cheerfully, "That young man never knew a stranger," I want to reply, "Yes, yes, you're on the right track. You've got a part of him all right," knowing that the larger thing cannot be broken down into its component parts without losing the whole. It is too big for us to talk about just now. Who wants to stand around at the end of a workday and make small talk about the hidden immensity of grace?

It often happens in a restaurant or a checkout line, when the woman (it is always a she) takes my credit card and asks me if I was his father. She is curious, that's all. "Say, were you *Adam's* father?" Her question inevitably opens onto a conversation about who they were in high school, what a charmer he was, and how sad it all is. It is a potentially exhausting conversation that neither of us really wants to pursue to its conclusion, because it has no conclusion that can be achieved in anything short of a lifetime.

So I simply reply, "Yep, I was. Still am."

So, "How's Adam?" the young man asks. The question simply will not go away. There are others still standing around us, but the event is quickly breaking up into separate conversations on the way to the bar. I put my hand on Marcus' elbow and steer him away from the traffic into a quiet corner of the room.

"Well, Adam has died," I say, making it sound as though it had happened yesterday. "I mean, he is dead." Too abrupt, especially for the young. "He developed cancer and passed away the summer before last. I am so sorry for you, Marcus. I mean, me telling you like this. This must be a terrible shock for you. I'm sorry I'm not doing a better job. You were friends."

"Oh," he replies, flatly. The smile is still there in anticipation of a happy story, but now it's exposed and foolish-looking. "I have to think about this. Adam passed. Wow. I don't know what to say."

"I never do either, but I've got to learn." We talk a little more about Adam's passing, share a stiff, shoulder-to-shoulder embrace, and he heads toward the elevators and his room.

I have never told a stranger about my son. I have received

words of comfort from people I don't know well, but I have never attempted to console anyone outside my family. Later, I realize I have said absolutely nothing to comfort him. To a young minister, no less, I have said not a word about Adam's goodness, his faith, his capacity for friendship, or my hope. Only that he is gone.

It occurs to me that I have acquired a new responsibility. I have become the interpreter of his death. God, I must do a better job.

The Rock

18

Toward the end of 2005 Tracy began looking for the dress. There were only so many places it could be: the storage room outside the kitchen, the upstairs closet in a plastic bag next to her wedding dress, or my grandmother's cedar chest at the foot of our bed. She found it in the chest.

Amidst a great company of saints and friends, we baptized Elizabeth Adam at Immaculate Conception Church. The "we" being the whole body of believers at the 9:30 Mass that day—including many young couples with their babies, some of the Latina girls from the school who had written Adam poems when he was sick, a few of the old hands from the daily Mass crowd, Jenny's entire family up from Charlotte and ours down from New Jersey, as well as twenty or twenty-five friends from the Divinity School who showed up because they believe in baptism and care about us.

Her baptism came not a moment too soon. Jenny had

postponed it until the winter because of my hospitalization. Now, with Elizabeth fairly bursting the lace around her neck and forearms, it was time.

The priest led the baptismal party up the aisle to the entrance of the sanctuary and to an enormous piece of granite bubbling with water. It was the same cool stone and restful sound that had comforted us during the previous summer, but now this rock would add its blessing to Jenny and Adam's child. When I thought of the summer of his dying and those hot afternoons when I slipped into the empty sanctuary to listen to the water, I remembered the story of the Israelites dying of thirst in the wilderness and how Moses struck the rock with his rod and water came pouring out. I stood beside Tracy and Sarah and Paul in the circle of family members as the priest performed the ceremony. He did not strike the rock, but I felt we were all renewed by the water that flowed from it.

When the priest said, "Elizabeth Adam, I baptize you in the name of the Father, and of the Son, and of the Holy Spirit," his words threw me into a time warp, and for a moment there I was baptizing my newborn son. The morning of his baptism had been sunny and crisp too, though much colder, and our joy was not tempered by the lethal significance of the sacrament. In 1972 we knew too little. In 2006 we knew too much. My old church's font was far less imposing than the monolith at Immaculate Conception, but it was water all the same. And Elizabeth Adam wore the same dress her daddy had worn, received the same name, and was marked with the same sign of suffering.

Today this child of earth approaches her father's realm

of light. Both are blessed, anointed, and clothed in white for purity. The earthiness of her second name, with all its intimations of mortality, is taken up into a new and glorious destiny. She will live—she will live. Long live Elizabeth Adam!

He must be so proud.

Nina wasn't there to voice her approval, so Tracy and I said it for her: "What a good strong name."

After the water, Elizabeth was anointed with oil. It was the first time her spiked hair laid down properly. She smelled like her father after the incense.

Then the priest invited all the children to come forward to give the newest member of the church a blessing. Cradled in Jenny's arms, she looked like a china doll with rouged cheeks and finely painted features. The children came and laid hands on baby Elizabeth. Too many hands, as it turned out. She enjoyed it for a while but then, in her beautiful white dress and with her hair and forehead glistening with oil, she began to sob.

After the service an older priest said to me, "It's the devil leaving when they wail like that." No, it is not, I thought. She is weeping for all that was lost to her before it was ever found. She is weeping because she understands what has just happened to her.

We virtually drowned her in a history of suffering, its memories bobbing along like debris in a swollen river. With her mom's help, she will memorize the stories and tolerate our need to tell and retell them. Until the day comes when she carefully takes the dress out of storage and brings her own child to the dangerous waters of this fountain.

. . .

On the day of her baptism, we took photographs of Elizabeth, Jenny, and the whole family, as we had done with Adam thirty-three years earlier, though this time with a better camera and more pleasing results. I have since bought a movie camera with which to make a record of Christmases and birthdays and other significant events. The quality of our new movies compares favorably to the faded and grainy Super 8s we have of Sarah and Adam bouncing in their cribs or of Tracy, blond hair flying in the wind, riding her bike in the country with one child on the bar, the other in the basket. I am twenty-nine in these productions, with dark hair, '70s sideburns, and a white t-shirt. I pick up the little boy and hold him above my head as if he were the Stanley Cup, then flip him onto my shoulders for a run to the lake. These Super 8s do not guard against death, any more than the still-puckered handkerchief with which I blotted his forehead long ago guarantees the benefits of baptism. They don't even qualify as memories at all, but only as visual aids to people like us who are prone to forgetfulness.

Who *were* the people in these portraits and what do you imagine these dusty artifacts once meant to them? The question arises whenever I walk into our windowless storage room and notice Sarah's doll collection or Adam's *dobok* hanging on a hook, as if waiting for another ferocious youngster to don it. Against the mutability of everyone and everything we ever loved, who will remember the ninety-five days of a young man's dying? Who will remember Adam after the few of us who mourn him are gone? Who will remember any of us after the waters have covered the earth again?

It is not a new question. Theoretical physicists have imagined the conservation of "information," perhaps in another universe where it might be preserved and reconstituted in a new form. But they don't explain *why* the universe would *want* to "remember itself." More than one of Israel's poets struggled with the same dilemma and begged God to "remember" the people. But it was the prophet Isaiah who provided a rationale for remembering by making a connection between memory and love: God will remember because God loves. He said God has written the names of his people on the palms of his hands and could no more forget them than a nursing mother can forget the baby at her breast.

The triumph of memory does not entail greater precision about the details of the past, but a deeply felt and enduring love, like the love of a nursing mother for her children. This is the love that sustains the cosmos and nourishes each of us on our journey through it. Not mementos and snapshots that remind us of love, but a love we are willing to risk in new relationships and with a new generation, "even at the cost of pain."

The many routines of the summer of 2005 are not forgotten, but they have passed into a deeper memory and no longer hold us as their occupied territory. The anointing, therapies, candlelit prayers, the intense days of suffering and preparation—all have given way to happier days of obligation that include swim lessons, playdates, spelling tests, and family outings at the beach. What remains among us is a new way of remembering in our family, something unexpected in 2005, and a love between a little girl and her mother that is something wondrous.

Now when Jenny takes Elizabeth "camping" they set up their tent and sleeping bags on the tiny gondola deck at the top of their house. It is the same platform high in the trees from which Elizabeth's mom and dad surveyed their future, counted the stars, and made the most of their fleeting summer nights.

Once she has had her bath and dried in the softest towel, she powders profusely, then puts on her plaid flannel nightie and white kneesocks. Her newly brushed strawberry hair hangs to her waist. She trots into our family room in that giddyap-horsey way children have of running and as usual makes a bee-line for the candles. She means for us to light every last one of them—sour apple, cinnamon, and honeydew melon, to name only a few of our flavors—and since she is our guest, we are happy to comply.

She hasn't been with us long before she lets us know it is time to visit the ancestors, the photographs of the ancestors, that is, arranged in cemetery-like rows on the cabinet beneath the towering bookshelves. We place her bottom firmly on the counter of the bookcase, and she shakes, handles, and rotates every photo with marsupial care. They are all there: great-grandfathers and great-grandmothers, grandfathers and grandmothers, aunts and uncles, cousins of every denomination, Baby Elizabeth, Mommy and Daddy. Some of us are dead, some are alive. Some of us she names, including Daddy; some she passes over with either an appreciative remark or a dismissive gesture.

It is twilight, but not a time of gathering gloom or sadness in this house. The sun is setting in the pine trees behind the neighbor's cabin. It leaves just enough light to do the things that require no light.

Like dancing.

The stereo sits very near the pictures on the next shelf. When she's finished with the photos, she gestures toward the possibility of music and the probability of dancing.

The woman of the house scoops the child into her arms as they begin to do a slow turn to the Mamas and the Papas. Cass Elliot is singing,

> *Sweet dreams till sunbeams find you*
> *Sweet dreams that leave all worries behind you*

The child likes this velvet voice, and she understands the important words. It's close enough to bedtime for her to savor her own sweet dreams, which she does luxuriously.

She smiles and opens her arms to the man of the house, and now the three of them are gliding and gently spinning around the hardwood floor while the whole gallery of ancestors looks on.

> *Stars shining bright above you*
> *Night breezes seem to whisper I love you*

The child smells of soap and incense.

The three of them have found yet another way to remember and forget at the same time. Dancing will do that when you dance with someone you love. The music eventually stops, night gently settles, and the ballroom turns to dust. But the dancers take no notice and dance on.

It has been seven years since he became one of the ancestors. That is how long it has been since I kissed his head and thanked him for being my son. I promised him then that his death would not ruin my life. It might have struck him as an odd thing to say, since self-devastation is widely regarded as the highest and most tragic form of grief. What I meant to convey to him was how utterly perverse it would be for a young man so filled with love to become the cause of an old man's bitterness.

God only knows how much we had left unsaid between us, but I badly wanted this final understanding with him.

At first, Adam appeared puzzled by my comment, and so I attempted to clarify: "Because, you know, the best thing that can happen to a father like me is to have a son like you. I promise you, my love, I will not waste this gift."

At that, he looked deeply into my eyes and nodded knowingly, but did not smile.

Acknowledgments

Writing a book is solitary work that should never be done alone. The few people in whom I confided my project all warned me about its emotional difficulty. They pursed their lips, as if they knew something about the dangers of remembering that I didn't understand. I spent solitary hours at my desk but wouldn't have made it to the finish line without the support of these friends and colleagues who looked out for me, took me to lunch, and asked me profound questions like "How's it going?" I'm thinking of Joel Marcus, Ellen Davis, Curtis Freeman, Peter Storey, Carol Shoun, Callie Davis, Grant Wacker, Maurice and Dotty Ritchie, Teresa Berger, Greg Jones, Don Ottenhoff, Jennifer Copeland, and Mary McClintock Fulkerson. William Wolfe, Robert Rideout, and Donald Whittier talked to me for hours about their friend Adam. Judge Frank R. Brown helped me by befriending my son and encouraging him in his work. Tracy and I were always able to call upon Bill Fulkerson, MD; Rev. Tom Colley; Rev. David McBriar, OFM; and Rev. Steve Patti, OFM. Russell Hall, MD, helped me understand the treatment of melanoma. Carolyn Richardson, Jenny Carroll, and Jean McInerney were unfailingly prompt and professional in providing trial transcriptions. My colleague Lauren Winner took time from her summer to read an early draft of the entire manuscript, offering critical advice and uncritical encouragement. A year later, Lil Copan worked through yet another draft. She did her best to help me understand what I was trying to do.

Institutional support came from Duke University in the form of a one-semester sabbatical leave. A generous grant from the Louisville Institute allowed me additional time to write. My special thanks go to Craig Dykstra of the Lilly Endowment and to James Lewis of the Institute. An additional grant from the Duke Divinity Institute on Care at the End of Life kept me working through an entire summer.

I owe a great deal to my quietly supportive agent, John F. Thornton of the Spieler Agency in New York City, and to my editor at Knopf, Caroline Zancan.

My daughter, Sarah, reinforced in me the sacredness of my responsibilities as a writer and a father. She has made me strong and made this a stronger and more honest book.

My most important readers are the four women in my family (and one of them won't read this for years): Tracy Kenyon Lischer, Sarah Kenyon Lischer, Jennifer Mary Lischer, and Elizabeth Adam Lischer. I dedicate this book to them in the comfortable knowledge that we all loved the same son, brother, husband, and father.

Finally, I am grateful to my son Adam for not "fleeing as a shadow," as the book of Job puts it, but for sticking with me and allowing me with his usual grace to speak openly of my love for him.

THE YEAR OF MAGICAL THINKING
by Joan Didion

Several days before Christmas 2003, John Gregory Dunne and Joan Didion saw their only daughter, Quintana, fall ill with what seemed at first flu, then pneumonia, then complete septic shock. She was put into an induced coma and placed on life support. Days later—the night before New Year's Eve—the Dunnes were just sitting down to dinner after visiting the hospital when John Gregory Dunne suffered a massive and fatal coronary. In a second, this close, symbiotic partnership of forty years was over. Four weeks later, their daughter pulled through. Two months after that, arriving at LAX, Quintana collapsed and underwent six hours of brain surgery at UCLA Medical Center to relieve a massive hematoma. This powerful book is Didion's attempt to make sense of the "weeks and then months that cut loose any fixed idea I ever had about death, about illness . . . about marriage and children and memory . . . about the shallowness of sanity, about life itself."

Memoir

NOTHING WAS THE SAME
by Kay Redfield Jamison

Kay Redfield Jamison, award-winning professor and writer, changed the way we think about moods and madness. Now Jamison uses her characteristic honesty, wit, and eloquence to look back at her relationship with her husband, Richard Wyatt, a renowned scientist who died of cancer. *Nothing Was the Same* is a penetrating psychological study of grief viewed from deep inside the experience itself.

Memoir